D0201480

RESTORATION

RETURNING
THE TORAH OF GOD
TO THE DISCIPLES
OF JESUS

D. THOMAS LANCASTER

RESTORATION

RETURNING
THE TORAH OF GOD
TO THE DISCIPLES
OF JESUS

D. THOMAS LANCASTER

FIRST FRUITS OF
ZION

Proclaiming the Torah and its way
of life, fully centered on Messiah,
to today's People of God

Copyright © 2005 by D. Thomas Lancaster. All rights reserved.
Publication rights First Fruits of Zion, Inc.

Publisher freely grants permission to reproduce short quotations in reviews, magazines, newspapers, websites or other publications. To reproduce, transmit or photocopy more than 400 words, please secure permission in writing from the publisher, which will be granted upon written request.

First Edition
First Printing, August 2005
Second Printing, September 2005
Third Printing, October 2005
Fourth Printing, May 2006 (Revised)
Fifth Printing, November 2007

Printed in the United States of America

Catalog Information: Theology
CBA Category Information: BST, DOT, OTT
ISBN: 1-892124-21-1

Unless otherwise noted, Scripture quotations taken from the New American Standard Bible®, Copyright © 1960, 1962, 1963, 1968, 1971, 1972, 1973, 1975, 1977, 1995 by The Lockman Foundation. Used by permission. (*www.Lockman.org*)

Cover Design: Avner Wolff
Cover image: Copyright © 2005 Israelimages / Kenneth Fisher

ATTENTION CHURCHES, SYNAGOGUES, STUDY GROUPS, TEACHERS AND OTHER ORGANIZATIONS: Quantity discounts are available on bulk purchases of this book for educational, fundraising or gift purposes, or as premiums for increasing magazine subscriptions or renewals. Special books or book excerpts can also be created to fit specific needs. Additionally, D. Thomas Lancaster and other First Fruits of Zion team members are available for speaking engagements, seminars and conferences. For more information or to arrange a speaking engagement, please contact First Fruits of Zion, PO Box 649, Marshfield, Missouri 65706-0649, USA. Phone (417) 468–2741 or (800) 775–4807. Email *www.ffoz.org/contact.*

First Fruits of Zion

PO Box 649
Marshfield, Missouri 65706-0649, USA
Phone (417) 468–2741 or (800) 775–4807
Fax (417) 468–2745
www.ffoz.org

Comments and questions: *www.ffoz.org/contact*

To Maria Anne

אשת חיל

and Soul Companion

And in loving memory of
Lorraine Delores Lancaster,
a true disciple of the King

CONTENTS

Foreword   ix

Prologue   1
     The Prophetic Return to Torah

1   My Journey to Torah   5
2   Our Journey Away from Torah   13
3   What Is the Torah?   29
4   Summing Up the Torah   37
5   Torah and the New Testament   47
6   The Giving of the Torah   57
7   The Inner Torah   67
8   The Sabbath of the Torah   75
9   The Festivals of Torah   89
10   The Life of Torah   101
11   The Jots and Tittles of Torah   113
12   The Difficult Laws of Torah   123
13   The Oral Torah   135
14   Paul and Torah   147
15   Res*Torah*ation   159

Appendix   165
     The Torah Club

Bibliography   173
Scripture Reference Index   175
Subject Index   179
Endnotes   185
Additional Resources   191

FOREWORD

Writing a book about God's Word is a serious undertaking, not to be entered into lightly. It comes with a weighty responsibility before God. The same can be said of publishing such a work. Therefore, it is with some consternation that we at First Fruits of Zion place this work before you. There are some risks involved. It is a dangerous business.

In the preface to his inspiring book *Birthright*, Professor David Needham points out, that any book about God's Word which challenges mainstream, conventional notions of faith and practice is risky primarily for two reasons. The first danger is that the book will become fuel for religious radicals whose greatest source of delight lies in iconoclasm. Such a person has an unhealthy love for overturning the theological tables of other believers. He gets a perverse charge out of labeling other people's sacred institutions as false or pagan, and feels smugly self-righteous when he does. He lives on radical teachings and leaps upon every opportunity to fracture harmony within his congregation and even within his own family.

But there is another risk, an even greater danger than fueling the misguided zealot. Because a book like this does challenge some of our most deep-seated, traditional Christian ideas, many sincere traditional Christians will reject it on this basis alone. Such a person is quick to shun any teaching that might force them to reexamine their understanding of biblical truth. Such a person might feel as if his narrow scope is a mark of special piety, and he will regard it as a religious duty to reject at first sight any suspicious teaching.

This book is intended for neither the iconoclast, nor the traditional Christian afraid to step outside of the box. This book is intended primarily for you—a believer who is committed to the authority of God's Word, even if it means rethinking a few deep-seated belief systems or reluctantly engaging in a little bit of iconoclasm. You are an independent thinker; a serious student of the Bible. You are not afraid to step outside of the proverbial box and be different, if that is what God calls you to do for Him. You are careful and deliberate in your assessment of Bible teaching—critical enough to know bunk when you see it, but open enough to explore unfamiliar ideas. Your faith, up to this point, has been a persistent quest for biblical truth, and the Holy Spirit has directed you in that quest thus far. You find no personal gratification in overturning the theological tables of other believers, but neither are you afraid of seeing your own table overturned—so long as it is Christ who does the overturning. Therefore, you will not be intimidated by what this writer has to say. You will weigh it, consider it, pray over it, and then make your decisions.

My prayer for you is that wherever Messiah might lead you—whether you agree with Daniel's conclusions or not—that your feet would be quick to follow.

May the Lord bless you and keep you!
Boaz Michael
Founder/President
First Fruits of Zion

Restoration is published by the ministry of First Fruits of Zion. First Fruits of Zion (FFOZ) is dedicated to proclaiming the Torah, its way of Life, fully centered on the Messiah, to today's people of God. Our work is grace based (Ephesians 2:8–10), Messiah centered (Luke 6:40, 1 John 5:1–5) and obedience oriented (Romans 3:31). FFOZ is a teaching ministry that produces books, magazines, in-depth reference commentaries, and teaching seminars. Our materials are intended to restore our faith and practice back to its original expression by looking at our faith from its proper historical and contextual setting. For more information on our work please visit our website at *www.ffoz.org* or call 1–800–775–4807 for samples of our literature.

PROLOGUE

THE PROPHETIC RETURN TO TORAH

Approximately 3,400 years ago, Moses saw the future. The book of Deuteronomy records his prophecies. He foresaw a time when the people of Israel would be exiled, scattered among the nations, driven from place to place, scorned, mocked, rejected, and persecuted. At every turn, history has proven his words. For nearly 2,000 years, the Jewish people have lived in exile. Wandering, bitterly oppressed, hated and reviled, homeless and hapless, a proverb and a taunt among all the people, in hunger, in thirst, and in the lack of all things, scattered from one end of the earth to the other, without rest and without a resting place, with trembling heart, failing eyes and despair of soul, in dread of night and heat of day, with no assurance of life, so that their very lives hung in doubt. Yet even the darkest and longest nights end with the dawning of a new day.

Moses foresaw a time of restoration when Israel's long night of exile would end. The sun would yet rise on Jacob. He said:

> The LORD your God will restore you from captivity, and have compassion on you, and will gather you again from all the peoples where the LORD your God has scattered you. If your outcasts are at the ends of the earth, from there the LORD your God will gather you, and from there He will bring you back. The LORD your God will bring you into the land which your fathers possessed, and you shall possess it. (Deuteronomy 30:3–5)

In the last half of the nineteenth century, the Jewish people began to return to their ancient homeland. In the middle of the twentieth century, the United Nations declared the modern state of Israel a nation. The ancient prophecy is being fulfilled. God is on the move. He is restoring His people.

But there is more to this restoration than Israel's return to her land. Moses went on to predict a return to Torah. He said, "And you shall again obey the Lord, and observe all His commandments which I command you today." (Deuteronomy 30:8) The commandments of which he speaks are those of the Torah.

The rest of the prophets of the Hebrew Scriptures confirmed the testimony of Moses. The dual return to the land and to Torah is a constant theme in the mouths of the prophets. Isaiah, Ezekiel, Jeremiah and all the other prophets concur. The people of Israel will return to the land and to the Torah.

Israel is returning to the land. Jewish immigrants arrive in modern-day Israel by the thousands every year. The return to Torah has begun as well. In the postmodern world, Jewish people everywhere are rediscovering the Torah. They are turning back to the ancient paths. They are rediscovering the Sabbath, the biblical festivals and the wealth of their eternal heritage. Modern Judaism calls this phenomenon the *Teshuvah* movement, a Hebrew word meaning "return."

In the last several decades, Orthodox Judaism has grown significantly as secular Jews return to faith. Even more astounding, for the first time since the days of the Apostles, tens of thousands of Jews have professed faith in Messiah—and that's a part of the return to Torah too. Deuteronomy 18:15 commands us to heed the Messiah. A full return to Torah requires a return to Messiah. A prophetic restoration is taking place. Jews are returning to the land. Jews are returning to the Torah. They are responding to the prompt and call of God's Spirit, and it is not just Jews who are feeling the call.

Around the world, spontaneously and simultaneously, believers are rediscovering the Torah. Even Gentile Christians are entering into the biblical Sabbath and keeping the biblical festivals. They are studying their Bibles in the light of Jewish sources. The seats of Messianic Jewish congregations are filling with Gentiles hungry to learn the Jewish roots of their faith. Even non-Messianic rabbis have noted the sudden influx of Torah-seeking Gentiles in their midst.

Is this just another evangelical fad? Or is this the fulfillment of the prophecy Moses made 3,400 years ago? For it shall come to pass that we shall again obey the Lord, and observe all His commandments, which Moses commanded us.

1

MY JOURNEY TO TORAH

THOMAS THE DOUBTER

I am a country pastor's son. The story is that when I was born, I surprised my parents with my gender. They already had three boys and two girls. They were expecting a third girl to balance out the family. Fully anticipating the birth of a daughter, they had picked out the name Sarah Joy for me. When I was born a male child, they were at a loss for what to name me. According to the story, a day or so after I was born, the Lord impressed upon my parents that my name was to be Daniel Thomas.

In truth, I have always preferred the Thomas side to the name because I identify more readily with the pragmatic, doubting disciple Thomas than I do with the mystical, vision-seeing prophet Daniel. In fact, doubt came to be one of the prime motivators in my life and studies, and to some degree, still is. Nevertheless, I am a believer, and have been since the age of four.

I grew up in a small, non-denominational, fundamentalist church that in later years came to be affiliated with the Evangelical Free Church of America. The church is called Swan Lake. It sat at the intersection of two country roads in the midst of endless miles of plowed prairie: fields of corn and soybeans as far as the eye could see. The lawn of the church was the only known piece of virgin prairie that remained in that flat land of big sky and wide horizons. The ruts of an old wagon road from pioneer times had left still-visible depressions in the grass crossing the property.

My father led Swan Lake until I was four years old. He set aside fulltime ministry in order to take a job that provided a more adequate income on which to raise six children. Yet he continued to be the most serious spiritual influence on my life, as he still is today. He is a man of great humility in possession of a great truth: the saving grace of the Gospel of Messiah. His greatest gift to me was the impartation of a solid grasp of that truth.

He was only the first in a long series of short-term pastors who came through our tiny rural church. At Swan Lake Evangelical Free Church, we taught the Gospel and generally believed ourselves to be the only outpost of true believers in the vicinity. We lived by the Bible—for the most part. While presenting sermons, our pastors often quipped, "Don't just take my word for it. Read the Bible yourself." I did.

As a young teen, I decided to read through the Bible. When I did, I noticed several glaring inconsistencies between the biblical text and church practice and theology. The words of Jesus were particularly unsettling. I began to have a sick feeling in my stomach. My church, which 'only did what the Bible said,' did not seem to have a great deal of affinity with actual biblical practice or theology.

Among the discrepancies I noted was the biblical Sabbath. I noticed that the Sabbath was the seventh day, Saturday, and there was nary a mention of a Sunday Sabbath for Christians. Still, I never considered the seventh day as relevant to Christians because, to me, Sabbath and church were synonymous, and church was always on Sunday. All the same, something was amiss. I felt the clouds of doubt gathering around me.

ACQUIRING A TEACHER

When I was a teenager, I went to Israel to visit my brother Steven, who was studying and teaching at the Institute of Holy Land Studies in Jerusalem. While touring Israel, we visited Jerusalem's *Yad V'Shem* Holocaust museum. It was my first real confrontation with the horror of the Holocaust. I was sixteen years old and was viewing the exhibits with a young history major from the Institute. The history student remarked, "No people on earth have been persecuted like the Jewish people." I quickly corrected him saying, "Except for the Christians." He laughed—a sound not often heard in *Yad V'Shem*. His laughter left me cold. As I looked into the eyes of the Nazis' victims in the photographs and stared through the photographically reproduced barbed-wire fences, I suddenly realized that I was on the wrong side of the fence. If we Christians were the real people of God, why were the Jews still targeted and hated by the world? Shouldn't we be the ones on whom the forces of evil bend their energy? Instead, we were the ones dispensing the evil. Something began to stir within me.

Shortly thereafter, my brother Steven returned from Israel to study toward his PhD in Semitic languages at the University of Wisconsin in Madison. While in Madison, he attended a Seventh Day Baptist Church. He and a fellow student (who also attended the Seventh Day Baptist Church) took it upon themselves to begin to welcome the Sabbath on Friday evenings in the traditional Jewish manner. When my parents and I visited my brother and his wife on a Friday evening, they brought in the Sabbath with the traditional lighting of candles, the bread, the wine, the blessings and the prayers of the Sabbath table. I was enamored with the richness of the tradition. My own religious experience, devoid of ritual, seemed to pale in comparison with this simple, eloquent expression of faith that was the Sabbath. Here was something of substance. I saw the Messiah in every ritual. The quiet, the peace and the spiritual essence of the Sabbath filled me with a strange nostalgia I could not explain.

My brother Steven has had a profound influence on me. Years later, when I began to study and teach the Bible, my brother's work in the biblical languages, the biblical text and biblical geography inspired me to read the Scriptures within a historical contextual frame of reference. He encouraged me to learn Hebrew, and he taught me how to handle the text responsibly. He tutored me in careful hermeneutics. When I was finishing college, he wrote independent studies in biblical Hebrew, literary criticism and Hebrew poetry. I studied his coursework for credit to finish my degree. Under his tutelage, I completed a course in biblical geography and was given the opportunity to study at the Institute of Holy Land Studies[1] on Mount Zion, Jerusalem, where he was a faculty member. He taught me about the land of Israel and the Scriptures of Israel. Whenever a passage of the Bible was under consideration, Steve pointed toward context: language, culture, geography and history. When I wanted to allegorize the real meaning away, he always pointed me back to the literal. He revolutionized my understanding of the Bible. He taught me the priority of Scripture. He showed me how the Torah is the foundation upon which all subsequent biblical revelation is built. He taught me that the Bible is supposed to make sense and that it actually does make sense. It is not a collection of disconnected mystical sayings and stray proof texts. It is real literature. He taught me that the Good Book really is a good book.

MESSIANIC JUDAISM

A few years before I began studying under my brother, I encountered Messianic Judaism. My wife and I visited a Messianic Jewish congregation. It was a strange, awkward experience. The congregation was a small fellowship—not more than a dozen people gathering on Sabbaths to learn Torah. Only one of them was Jewish, and it wasn't the rabbi. It was an odd collection of people, but it was there that we began to learn Torah from a Messianic perspective. In one month there, I learned more from the Bible than I had in all my years at church. We learned about the authentic roots of Christianity. We learned about the Sabbath and the biblical festivals. I began to see Yeshua, the real, biblical Jesus—the Jewish Jesus—and I began to understand Him in His Jewish context. It was eye opening. It was like reading the Scriptures for the very first time.

The thrill of discovery was exhilarating. At first, I assumed that our family and the few people attending the congregation with us were the only people in the whole world who understood the Scriptures this way. Then we discovered a ministry called First Fruits of Zion (FFOZ) and realized that we were not alone. The materials of FFOZ were like water in the desert.

Torah study was eye-opening, revolutionary, explosive and thrilling. It was an antidote to doubt, and it fueled me on to study all the more. My misgivings about the Bible began to vanish. The more I studied the Torah and the Jewishness of Jesus and the early believers, the more the Thomas side of me was confounded.

If you have not yet had the opportunity to learn the Bible from the Hebrew Roots perspective, you will not understand what I mean. Terms like eye-opening, faith-building and head-exploding all fall short of describing the joy of reading and studying the Scriptures in their Jewish context. Not that this should be surprising. After all, the Bible is a thoroughly Jewish book. How we Christians ever hoped to understand the Bible without understanding the Torah and Judaism, I do not know.

Imagine a person who has grown up with blurred vision. He assumes that everyone sees the world in the same blurry, hazy, indistinct shapes that he does. He assumes that blurriness is normal. He does not know he is missing anything. Then one day he is given a pair of corrective lenses. Immediately the world takes on sharp definition. He realizes how much he has been missing. Studying the Bible through a Jewish/Torah perspective is a lot like that.

It was a revolutionary journey for me. The whole Hebrew Roots perspective was life saving because, in many ways, it salvaged my faith—a real restoration.

DANIEL THE JUDAIZER?

Within two years we left the Messianic Jewish world, and I began to study Torah in earnest in the context of Orthodox Judaism. I immersed myself in the world of traditional Jewish literature. I devoured Torah, *Talmud*, *Midrash* and classical Jewish commentary on the Bible. I remember how my heart would burn within me as the rabbi expounded on the Torah. In every word he said, in every passage we studied, it seemed the very image of Messiah stepped forth in brilliant colors. At times I felt that I would burst from the excitement. I've never felt closer to the Master than when studying Torah in the midst of His people.

I emerged from those years with a passion to bring Torah to my brothers and sisters in Christ. I took positions teaching adult Christian education classes in large evangelical churches. Other teaching opportunities opened, and soon I was teaching in churches and Messianic Jewish congregations as many as four to five times a week. It was through these various teaching opportunities that I received the dubious honor of being dubbed a 'Judaizer.'

What is a Judaizer? In the next chapter, we will see that according-ing to the way that many of the Church Fathers and reformers would define the term, I am a Judaizer. That does not mean that I want to make converts for Judaism, nor does it mean that I am trying to make Christians Jewish. It simply means that I am encouraging Christians to return to what I understand to be the original form of Christianity. I am teaching Christians that God's laws, in one fashion or another, apply to them.

The classic church understands a Judaizer as one who compels Christians to adopt Jewish practices, such as observance of the Sabbath and the biblical festivals. According to that definition of the word, I'm a Judaizer.

Note that the biblical term "Judaizer" is different. In the Bible, a Judaizer is someone who teaches that a Gentile must convert to Judaism through the auspices of a ritual circumcision in order to be saved. When Peter separated from the Gentile believers in Antioch, he did so under pressure of Jewish believers from Jerusalem who believed that Gentiles were not worthy of table fellowship, much less salvation, unless they converted to Judaism. Paul regarded this as heretical and accused Peter of Judaizing.[2] Paul wrote his epistle to the Galatians to refute the Judaizing believers at work within the Galatian community.

◊ Conventional definition of a Judaizer: One who compels Christians to adopt Jewish practices, such as observance of the Sabbath and the biblical festivals.

◊ Biblical definition of a Judaizer: One who compels non-Jews to undergo a ritual conversion in order to merit salvation, whereby they are reckoned as Jewish proselytes.

According to the biblical definition, I am not a Judaizer. I do not believe in compelling non-Jews to undergo a ritual conversion whereby they are reckoned as Jewish proselytes.

I believe that "by grace you have been saved through faith; and that not of yourselves, *it is* the gift of God; not as a result of works, so that no one may boast." (Ephesians 2:8–9) I do not believe in keeping the law in order to be saved. I believe in keeping it because

I am saved. Nonetheless, that belief makes me, according to the conventional definition of the term, a Judaizer.

DANIEL THE LEGALIST?

Not only am I a Judaizer, I am a legalist. How does a person become a legalist? What is a legalist?

Once again, there is the conventional definition of legalism and then there is the theological definition. In conventional usage, a legalist is anyone who believes that he or others should keep a particular law or commandment from the Bible that is no longer practiced in the church. For example, if a pastor were to tell the teenagers in his congregation that they should not get tattoos because Leviticus 19:28 forbids it, that would be regarded as a legalistic interpretation. The young people in his youth group would probably charge him with being a legalist. (I know of a situation where this actually occurred.) I believe that getting a tattoo is wrong, so that makes me a legalist. But I am not a legalist in the biblical sense.

Legalist is not a biblical word, but it is a biblical idea. In the Bible, a legalist is essentially the same as a Judaizer. It is someone who teaches that we must keep the commandments of God in order to merit His grace, affection, favor and ultimately salvation. Surprisingly, the legalists were not the Pharisees; they were believers who taught salvation through works. They were Paul's opponents.

I am not that kind of legalist. I am a big fan of the Apostle Paul's writings. Let me state it again. I believe that "by grace you have been saved through faith; and that not of yourselves, *it is* the gift of God; not as a result of works, so that no one may boast." (Ephesians 2:8–9) To me, that means that I have no personal merit sufficient to earn God's favor, nor can I generate it. I do not believe in keeping the law in order to be saved or even to maintain salvation. But I do believe in keeping it because I am saved. That belief makes me, according to the conventional definition of the term, a legalist.

◊ Conventional definition of Legalist: One who compels Christians to live by a certain standard or commandment of Scripture that is no longer generally practiced in the church.

◊ Theological definition of Legalist: One who attempts to earn salvation through obedience to the law.

According to the biblical parameters as expressed in Paul's epistles, I am not a legalist, nor am I a Judaizer. But according to the conventional use of the terminology, I am both. The rest of this book explains why.

DANIEL THE HERETIC?

In some circles, I will be regarded as worse than a legalist and Judaizer; I will be seen as a heretic. According to many Christian authorities, teaching Christians to keep the biblical laws of Torah is heresy. Wow! How does a person become a heretic? Probably by reading books like this one.

Let me encourage you to keep reading anyway. In the study of Torah, the conclusion is sometimes less important than the process of study because the study of Torah requires study of God's Word. If you have read even this far, it is because you are a unique, exceptional person. You have a passion for truth and a serious concern for your faith in God. You have a desire to discern between God's truth and man's errors. You may be under the suspicion that this very book is one of man's errors, and it could well be. But how will you know if you don't study it out? As my pastors always told me, "Don't just take my word for it. Read the Bible yourself."

It was good advice. It changed my life.

If, after reading the rest of this book, you do not reach the same (seemingly heretical) conclusions I have, you will nevertheless be better prepared to give an answer when you encounter other legalists and Judaizers like me.

2

OUR JOURNEY AWAY FROM TORAH

THE GOSPEL IN EXILE

The Jewish people have lived in exile since the age of the Apostles. So has the Gospel.

Like the Jewish people, the Gospel began in the land of Israel. Like the Jewish people, the Gospel spread out into every nation during times of great persecution. Like the Jewish people, the Gospel now resides among the nations of the *Diaspora*. It is as if the Gospel is in exile because, like the Jewish people, it has been removed from its context and disconnected from its point of origin. We Gentile Christians have in some ways misunderstood and misapplied the Gospel because we have been ignorant of the Jewish origin and Torah context of the Gospel.

These years of exile have been productive for both the Jewish people and the Gospel. Like the Jewish people in exile, the Gospel has flourished. Like the Jewish people in exile, it has entered every nation and every culture on the globe. Like the Jewish people in exile, the Gospel has impacted the entire world.

But the time is nigh for the exile to come to an end.

Moses foresaw a time of restoration. He foresaw a time when the people of Israel would return from exile and turn back to the commandments of God. "And you shall again obey the Lord, and observe all His commandments which I command you today." (Deuteronomy 30:8) One component of that restoration is certainly a return to the Gospel of Messiah. Now, at the culmination of the ages, Jews are returning to the land. They are returning to the

Torah. In a similar way, they are returning to the Gospel, and the Gospel itself is returning from exile. New Testament scholars are returning the Gospel to its Torah context and reconnecting it with its Jewish origins. Let me explain what I mean.

In the days of the Apostles, Christianity was not yet a separate religion from Judaism. An honest reading of the New Testament from a biblical-Jewish perspective makes it clear that the first-century church never thought of herself as separate and excluded from Judaism. Rather, she considered herself as part of the whole of Israel. She never imagined herself as replacing Judaism. She might have conceived of herself as a reform within Judaism, but not as a separate entity.

The writings of the Apostles assume the believers to be a sect within the larger religion of Judaism. Jesus was actually a Jewish teacher of Torah. His Hebrew name—that is, His real name—was Yeshua. He kept the Torah, taught the Torah, and lived by the Torah. He taught His disciples to keep the Torah in imitation of Him. He argued with the teachers of other sects of Judaism. He denounced the Sadducees, rebuked the Pharisees and brought correction to errant teachings, but He did not institute a new religion, nor did He cancel the Torah. Instead, He sought to bring restoration to the ancient faith of Abraham, Isaac and Jacob. He diligently sought after the lost sheep of Israel—those who had turned away from Torah. He affirmed the words of Moses and brought clarification regarding the proper observance of God's Law. His followers, the Apostles and the believers, also remained within the parameters of normative, first-century Jewish expression. They met daily in the Temple. They congregated in synagogues. They proclaimed the Scriptures of Israel. They kept the biblical festivals, the Sabbaths, the dietary laws and the whole of Torah as best they were able.

When non-Jews began to enter the faith through the ministry of Paul of Tarsus, they too congregated in synagogues and embraced the standards of biblical Judaism. They understood themselves to be "grafted in"[3] to Israel and made citizens of the larger "commonwealth of Israel."[4] They were allowed certain dispensations. Ritual conversion through circumcision was not required of them. Neither were they required to forsake their ethnic identity and 'become Jewish.' Yet their faith was the faith of Israel, placed in the Messiah of Israel, and they henceforth practiced the religion of Israel. But things were changing.

The inclusion of Gentiles in the big tent of Judaism was unpopular. Jewish authorities in local synagogues pressured the non-Jews to undergo formal conversion. So did many of the Jewish believers. In his epistles, Paul argued vociferously for the right of non-Jews to be recognized as "fellow heirs" with Israel.[5]

At the end of the book of Acts, we see a picture of the Yeshua movement still in the cradle of Judaism, still a sect within it. It is about the year 65 AD, Paul was a prisoner in the city of Rome and ministering to the believers there. Within two years, Paul went to meet the Master when Nero the Emperor had him beheaded. Nero began an open persecution against the believers, blaming them for the burning of Rome. A short time later, Peter too found martyrdom in Rome when Nero had him crucified. Nero then added to his infamy by launching a massive military campaign against the Jewish state. He sent the dreaded Tenth Legion, under the famous General Vespasian, to put down the revolt in Judea. Suddenly, Jews were regarded as enemies of the state.

After Nero died and Vespasian was made emperor, Vespasian's son Titus carried on the war by bringing the Roman army against Jerusalem. Our brothers and sisters in Jerusalem heeded the words of the Master. He had forewarned them, saying:

> When you see Jerusalem surrounded by armies, then recognize that her desolation is near. Then those who are in Judea must flee to the mountains, and those who are in the midst of the city must leave, and those who are in the country must not enter the city; because these are days of vengeance, so that all things which are written will be fulfilled. (Luke 21:20–22)

The armies came and the believers fled. The Roman legions destroyed the city of Jerusalem and burned the Temple. The Jewish believers in Judea and Jerusalem either fled east across the Jordan River or were carried off into captivity and sold as slaves along with their countrymen. In one sense, the Gospel went into exile with them, scattered among the nations.

Separating from Judaism

The Jewish War gave rise to the politics of anti-Semitism. Imagine a Gentile believer living in the Roman colony of Philippi, attending a Jewish worship service on the Jewish day of worship and keeping Jewish rituals when suddenly his nation goes to war with the Jews. Previously he might have been known simply as 'Tony the Believer' from Philippi. Subsequent to the revolt his neighbors began to refer to him as 'Tony the Jew lover, enemy of the state' from Philippi, or even just 'Tony the Jew.'

Emperor Vespasian followed up the Jewish War by imposing a heavy, punitive annual tax upon all Jewish households in the empire. He determined Jewish households as those who worshipped after the Jewish manner. With the addition of the *Fiscus Judaicus* tax, Gentile believers had financial, political and cultural incentives to distance themselves from Judaism.[6]

Shortly after the Jewish War and the destruction of Jerusalem, synagogues throughout the world introduced a new benediction in the daily liturgies that was actually a curse on believers in Yeshua and other heretics.[7] The synagogue authorities expelled worshippers who would not pray the curse. Thus the believers found themselves expelled from the Jewish assembly. The Master had foreseen this. He warned His disciples that "they will make you outcasts from the synagogue." (John 16:2)

The Gentile pagans resented the non-Jews because they were essentially Jewish. The Jewish authorities resented them because they were believers. Excommunication from the synagogue was deeply offensive and created sharp animosity toward Jews (even among Jewish believers), who were already none too popular throughout the empire. What is worse, the expulsion left believers with no place to assemble on the Sabbath, or to assemble at all.

Years went by as the church, now largely dominated by Gentiles, struggled to identify herself. Heresies and persecutions plagued her throughout those formative years. Around the turn of the century, the new emperor, Domitian, the son of Vespasian, afraid of another Jewish revolt, unleashed a series of new persecutions against the believers—again because of their Jewish association. In that wave of persecutions, John, the last Apostle, was exiled to Patmos.

Put yourself in the sandals of the average non-Jewish believer. On the one hand, the synagogue has thrown you and your family out because you are offensive to Judaism. On the other hand you are seeing your friends and family imprisoned, even tortured and killed, because they are being identified with the Jewish religion. You are guilty by association with a religion that doesn't want you associating with them.

THE SECOND CENTURY

By the time the second century began, anti-Jewish sentiment was so high in the church (especially the Roman church) that most non-Jews no longer wanted to be identified with Jews at all. The first-century believers were long dead and gone. A new generation had been raised to view Jews and even Jewishness as the antithesis of Christianity. It is not unlike the bitter hostility many Protestants hold for Catholics. It fills some deep psychological need to define oneself against something. Unfortunately, that 'something' is often one's parents, which is what Catholics were to Protestants—and what Judaism was to Christianity.

Theologically, the church leaders decided that the Christian church had replaced the Jews as the true Israel of God. They decided that they were now the true people of God, and that Jews were consigned to damnation and everlasting cursedness from God.

The new generation (second century) was the generation that lived through the Second Jewish Revolt. In the third decade of the second century, the Jews of Judea revolted against Rome again, this time during the days of the pagan Emperor Hadrian. They banded together under the leadership of the rebel warrior Shimon Bar Kokba. Rabbi Akiva declared him to be messiah. All of Bar Kokba's men were told that they must swear allegiance to his messiahship, even proving their allegiance by maiming themselves for him. Their refusal to declare Bar Kokba as the Messiah surely alienated the last Jewish believers among the Jews of Israel. It was the last break between the believers and Judaism.

Of course, Bar Kokba was not the messiah. Rome quickly crushed his rebellion. Jerusalem was again destroyed, and the Jews again faced imperial persecution. The Talmud calls it the Age of the Great Persecution. In those days, Emperor Hadrian made laws declaring it illegal to keep the Sabbath, to ordain rabbis and to practice Judaism. Believers could be arrested for keeping the laws of Torah. Those who did were arrested and martyred along with the faithful among the Jewish people. Rome made no distinction between Jews and believers practicing the Jewish faith. To survive, it became necessary for believers to further disassociate from Judaism. Unfortunately, Paul's compiled letters, when read outside their original context, provided ample justification for that disassociation. The emerging Christian movement read Paul's arguments for the inclusion of Gentiles in the Kingdom backward to imply the exclusion of Torah.

THE CHURCH FATHERS

We call the leaders of the generation of Gentile believers who lived through the Second Jewish Revolt the Church Fathers. They were godly men doing the best they could with the understanding they had. Unfortunately, their understanding of Torah was largely a misunderstanding. One of the Church Fathers, Ignatius, wrote an epistle to the congregations of Asia (where John had lived and served just three decades before). He said to them:

> Let us therefore no longer keep the Sabbath after the Jewish manner, and rejoice in days of idleness…But let every one of you keep the Sabbath in a spiritual manner… not in relaxation, not in eating things prepared the day before, not in finding delight in dancing and clapping which have no sense in them.[8]

What did he mean? Why did he have to prohibit second-century believers from keeping the Sabbath? He had to prohibit them because despite all the adversity, John's and Paul's congregations were still keeping Sabbath.

In the same era, men like the author of the epistle of Barnabas arose. The epistle of Barnabas is a known forgery that is alleged to be written by Barnabas, Paul's traveling companion. It is actually a deeply misguided, anti-Semitic justification for replacement theology. The author of this pseudo-epistle describes the Jews as wretched men deluded by an evil angel (that is, the God of the Hebrew Scriptures) and abandoned by God. In the epistle of Barnabas, the laws of Torah are allegorized and Judaism is condemned.

It was in this era that we have the first record of Christians proselytizing Jews. There is a famous Christian-Jewish dialogue in the form of a polemic between a Hellenist Jew named Trypho and the Church Father Justin Martyr. It is a testament to how far the Roman believers had already divorced themselves from Judaism and even from the Scriptures. Justin Martyr explained to Trypho (and all the Jews) that the Torah was given to Jews as a punishment for their exceptional wickedness and because of God's special hatred for the Jewish people. He said, "We, too, would observe your circumcision of the flesh, your Sabbath days and in a word all your festivals, if we were not aware of the reason why they were imposed upon you, namely, because of your sins and your hardness of heart." Yet even Justin Martyr admitted that, in his day (153 CE), there were believers who still practiced the laws of Torah, both Jewish and non-Jewish believers. These "weak-minded" brothers, he reluctantly conceded, were still saved, despite their foolish insistence on observing the laws of Moses.[9]

At the same time that men like Ignatius and Justin Martyr were holding their sway over the developing church, the believers saw the rise of the great heretic Marcion. He came sweeping through the church with his refined doctrine that the Jesus of the New Testament had defeated and unseated the evil god of the Jews. Therefore, the Hebrew Scriptures (what we call the Old Testament) and any Jewish relics in the Christian faith needed to be expelled. He compiled the first version of the 'New Testament.' Marcion's Bible consisted of portions of the book of Luke and ten of Paul's epistles, which he edited to remove what he termed "Jewish corruptions." He discarded the rest of the books of the Apostles, as well as the entire Old Testament, on the basis of their Jewishness. Marcion's anti-Jewish, anti-Torah version of Christianity caught on quickly. Though the Roman church denounced him as a heretic in 144 CE, Marcionite churches, bishops and communities sprang up throughout the empire. Tertullian compared the Marcionites to "swarms of wasps building combs in imitation of the bees."[10] He was wildly popular and stunningly influential, and his teachings remained deeply rooted—even after he was denounced for his heresies.

RESURRECTION SUNDAY

Meanwhile an annual remembrance of the resurrection of Messiah had emerged in Christian practice. It occurred every year on the Sunday that followed Passover. The Roman Christians called it Easter, an older name for a pagan Roman springtime festival. The Roman church ordered believers to quit reckoning Passover by the traditional Jewish method and to only keep this annual resurrection festival. It was a great controversy because the churches of Asia (the congregations of Paul and John) did not want to play ball with Roman authority. They wanted to keep Passover as they always had. But in the end the authority of Rome prevailed.

Part of the fallout of the controversy was that Sunday was elevated while all the biblical (i.e., Jewish) elements, festivals and days were eliminated. It became a Christian innovation to fast on the Sabbath and rejoice on Sunday as a weekly celebration of the annual Sunday resurrection festival. The church began to celebrate Sunday as a weekly, mini-Roman, Easter.

CONSTANTINE AND NICEA

By the time Constantine converted to Christianity and declared it the official state religion, most of the Jewish elements were gone. Except for hold-out sects of Jewish believers like the Nazarenes and the Ebionites, the observance of Torah had been largely eliminated from the faith. Constantine made the divorce from Judaism final with the Council of Nicea (325 CE). His official policy regarding Torah observance is expressed in his words: "Let us have nothing in common with the detestable Jewish rabble."[11] The decisions made at Nicea defined the course the church would take henceforth. Later church councils followed suit, and new legislation was introduced to forbid Christians from observing Torah. The Council of Antioch (341 CE) prohibited Christians from celebrating Passover with the Jews, while the Council of Laodicea (363 CE) forbade Christians from observing the biblical Sabbath. The edicts of these various councils make it clear that many believers were still, even in the fourth century, keeping Torah.

In the late fourth century, John Chrysostom delivered a series of sermons in Antioch against the Jews and against the Judaizers among the Christians. "Judaizer" is a term that the Church Fathers applied to anyone who practiced the laws of Torah. Chysostom's sermons contained an abundance of hateful, anti-Jewish venom. He singled out the observance of Torah as a disease in Christianity.

> What is this disease? The festivals of the pitiful and miserable Jews are soon to march upon us one after the other and in quick succession: the Feast of Trumpets, the Feast of Tabernacles, the fasts [i.e., the Day of Atonement]. There are many in our ranks who say they think as we do. Yet some of these are going to watch the festivals and others will join the Jews in keeping their feasts and observing their fasts. I wish to drive this perverse custom from the church right now...But now that the Jewish festivals are close by and at the very door, if I should fail to cure those who are sick with the Judaizing disease...[they] may partake in the Jews' transgressions." [12]

Chrysostom went on to denounce Christians who participated in the festivals, the Sabbath and the dietary laws. He rebuked them for attending the synagogue. In total, he delivered eight consecutive sermons on the subject, ample testimony that even in the fourth century many believers were still obedient to Torah. Yet in the end, the will of the Church Fathers prevailed, and the divorce between Christianity and the Torah of Moses was completed.

These things had been foreseen. The Master warned His disciples that, in the troubled times to come, "Many will fall away...False prophets will arise and will mislead many. Because lawlessness is increased...." (Matthew 24:10–12) Paul had warned the Ephesian elders that "after my departure savage wolves will come in among you, not sparing the flock; and from among your own selves men will arise, speaking perverse things, to draw away the disciples after them." (Acts 20:19–30) In writing to the Thessalonians, he warned them of an apostasy to come, an apostasy of Torahlessness: "Let no one in any way deceive you, for *it will not come* unless the apostasy comes first…For the mystery of lawlessness is already at work." (2 Thessalonians 2:3, 7)

As time went on, and the Dark Ages began, the Christian church turned violent toward the Jewish people. Synagogues and holy books were burned, whole communities were slaughtered. Jewish men and women were tortured—all in the name of Christ. The pages of church history are stained red with the spilled blood of the Jewish people.

The church tightened her grip on her own people by forbidding laity from possessing a copy of the Scriptures. The Holy Book was forbidden. A person caught with a copy of the Scriptures could be sentenced to death. Like the Jewish people, the Gospel was truly in exile, lost among the nations.

The Reformation

Almost 500 years ago, the return from exile began. I want to take you back there for a moment. Imagine yourself in Germany, a German Christian, in the year 1517. When you attend church, you go into a beautiful building with high stone spires and vaulted ceilings, stained glass and marble, candlelit masses, monks chanting in Latin, a priest to hear your confession, another priest to sing the mass, incense and votives, Mary, the baby Jesus, Saint Peter, Saint Paul, Saint Ann, and the Holy Father in Rome. The masses are inspiring. The architecture is captivating. The liturgy is lofty, high and holy. We have come a long way from the simple, first-century sect of Judaism that proclaimed the man from Nazareth to be resurrected from the dead.

But there are some things amiss here. The mass proclaiming the mystery of Christ is beautiful—but you can't understand a word of it, unless you have a university education and can speak Latin, which isn't likely. The pictures of the Madonna, the Christ Child, Saint Peter and Saint Paul are as much of the Scripture as you are likely to really know because there is no Bible available for the common person. Bibles are all written in Latin, and the laity is forbidden to possess a copy.

When you go to the priest to say your confession, there is a charge. You are expected to pay for forgiveness. For an extra donation you can buy grace for dead relatives to release them from torment faster. Relief sculptures, mocking and ridiculing the Jewish people, are carved right into the architecture of the church. This is what you know about the Jews. Utter contempt and utter disdain.

But listen to that pounding sound.

Outside the door, someone is standing on a ladder. He is nailing something to the door. It is the year 1517, the year Martin Luther, a disillusioned Augustine monk from the Black Monastery in Erfert, nailed his Ninety-five Theses to the church door in Wittenberg.

If you take the time to read his Ninety-five Theses, it may surprise you to discover how benign it is. This is not a list of radical reforms that Luther sought to impose on the church. It is not a statement against the authority of the papacy or Rome, an indictment of images or the worship of saints. It does not call into question the theology of worshipping Mary as the mother of God. It is not very radical at all. It is a continuous sustained argument against the selling of indulgences—that is, charging people for grace and forgiveness.

But it was enough. Someone had dared to question the authority of the church to impose its own man-made rituals and doctrines. Someone had dared to say, "Hey, wait a second. That's not in the Bible. That's not part of the original Christian faith."

Once that point had been made, there was no way to stop the inevitable. Thanks to Gutenberg, it was not long before Bibles were being printed in common languages so that anyone who wanted could read what was written. The average person could read and understand the stories in the Gospels, the words of the Master, the words of Paul, and the whole of the Scriptures. We call it the Protestant Reformation.

But did Luther go far enough? Clearly the myriad daughter denominations of the Protestant Reformation do not think so. Each subsequent Protestant movement has contributed its own set of further reforms. Ostensibly, each reform is an attempt to reach further back to the original first-century church of Yeshua and His disciples.

The effort to return to the first-century church is praiseworthy. It comes from a desire to conform our lives and congregations to the authority of the Word of God. The motives of these reformers are pure and good. Their methodology, however, has been flawed. An important piece of the puzzle is missing.

What the various Protestant reformers have failed to recognize about the first-century church is that she was Jewish. She was a part of first-century Judaism. Yeshua, the disciples, the first believers, the worship system, the Scriptures, the interpretation of the Scriptures, the teaching, the vernacular and even the very concepts of faith and grace, Messiah and God were all patently Jewish.

Any attempt at church reformation, any attempt to return to the original New Testament church falls short as long as it refuses to acknowledge the essential Jewishness of our faith.

Why did the Protestant Reformation stop where it did? If it was really all about throwing out the unbiblical church traditions that had tainted Christianity, why did it retain the Roman calendar and Roman theologies? Why do Protestant churches still call Sunday the Sabbath and eat ham on Easter instead of unleavened bread on Passover?

It seems that during Luther's lifetime, hopes were high in the Jewish community that the Protestant Reformation would put a stop to Christian persecution of the Jewish people. In fact, the opposite happened. Martin Luther issued an encyclical called *Against the Sabbath Keepers* and another one called *Against the Judaizers.* In these papers, he admonished Protestant Christians for keeping Sabbath and adopting Jewish customs. In 1543, Luther published *On the Jews and Their Lies*, in which he advocated burning down synagogues in every town and forcing Jews to convert or die.

What was the reason for his rage against the Jewish community? Most scholars agree that he was disappointed that Jews did not embrace Protestant Christianity. He had hoped the Jews would share his excitement over stripping back Roman Catholic tradition. When they did not respond with mass conversions, he turned against them. But another part of his ire arose from things that were happening within his own movement. The Protestants were reading their Bibles and concluding that authentic, biblical Christianity was indeed Jewish. They were returning to Jewish practices, returning to Torah, keeping Sabbath and festivals. The result was even more bitter persecution by the reformers to try to stop the 'Judaization' of the Protestant movement.

It is true. The Renaissance Age boasted a strong Hebrew Roots movement.

As early as 1538, just 21 years after the Wittenberg door incident, Oswald Dlaidt and Andreas Fischer launched a radical return to the Hebrew roots of the faith from within the Anabaptist church of Moravia. Fisher translated Jewish liturgy out of the Hebrew for use in services and even went so far as to write a Christian *Siddur*, essentially a translation of the Jewish prayer book. Once again believers were praying the ancient blessings before eating and offering thanks after meals and praying the basic prayers of the Jewish expression. It was against these Moravian Hebrew Rooters that Luther wrote *Against the Sabbath Keepers*, which condemned Sabbath observance as sinful. By means of stiff resistance from Luther and persecution from the larger Protestant world, the Moravian Torah movement was stopped.

A reformer by the name of Paul Fagius gave a historical interpretation of the New Testament by explaining the Lord's Supper in the context of Passover and the sayings of Yeshua in the context of rabbinic literature. Luther and his associates labeled him a Judaizer. For Luther and his followers, refuting the radical reformation became synonymous with rejecting Judaizers. The reformation was spinning out of control and, in some places, rapidly returning to Jewish form and practice.

Wherever the Bible was read without theological manipulation, believers were returning to Torah. In the end, however, the Protestants largely prevailed. The return to Torah was stifled. The Gospel would remain in exile. The time was not yet ripe. Several more centuries would pass before the momentum returned.

END OF THE EXILE

From 1938 to 1945, the Jewish people endured a seven-year great tribulation, the culmination of the horrors of exile. The long years of persecution reached a demonic crescendo. Blackness. Utter despair. Ruin in the face of naked evil. Six million dead. Yet the people of Israel lived.

As the world emerged from the travails of World War II, stories of the Holocaust began to circulate. Slowly, the realization sank in. Christians all over the world began to understand what had happened. Theologians and churchmen were abashed to realize that their own religious prejudices and bigotry had contributed to the greatest human travesty of all time.

Though he was a self-proclaimed pagan, Hitler justified the genocide by pointing to Christian writings and Christian history. He even quoted Luther. "Whole libraries of books have been published which show how Hitler translated Luther's ideas into action."[13] Ashamed and mortified, Christian thinkers and theologians began to publicly swear off anti-Semitism. As a part of that process, they reexamined old church theologies that had allowed for and even encouraged the historic brutalization of the Jewish people. Bible scholars began to reexamine the assumption that the church had replaced the Jewish people. They also reexamined the assumption that Jews are cursed by God and enemies of Christ. This process was the beginning of a renaissance in Christian thought and theology. A new breed of scholars emerged, willing to examine the origins of Christianity in light of Jewish sources. We are only now beginning to reap the harvest of post-Holocaust biblical research.

At the same time, two other remarkable events added momentum to the return to biblical Christianity. Sometime in late 1946 or early 1947, Muhammed edh-Dhib ("The Wolf") and two of his cousins from the Ta'amirah Bedouin tribe were seeking a stray goat when they discovered the mouth to a cave near the Dead Sea. Throwing a stone into the cave, they heard the sound of breaking pottery inside. They later returned to the cave and discovered several clay jars. Three of them contained ancient scrolls, including scrolls of the prophet Isaiah. At the time the boys did not understand the value of their find.

They had discovered what would come to be called the Dead Sea Scrolls. The Dead Sea Scrolls are an ancient library of biblical and Jewish religious literature dating from the days of the Apostles. They have revolutionized the way we understand first-century Judaism and the origins of Christianity.

In March of 1947, these Bedouin boys sold the scrolls to Kahil Iskander Shahin, a shoemaker in Bethlehem, presumably so that he might utilize the parchment in his trade. Kahil recognized that the documents were ancient and perhaps valuable. He sold four of them to Mar Athanasius Samuel of St. Mark's Monastery in Jerusalem. Professor Eleazar Sukenik of Hebrew University was allowed to see the scrolls and attempted to purchase them, but Mar Samuel did not want to sell the scrolls to the professor.

Sukenik disguised himself and made a secret trip to Arab Bethlehem to pay a visit to Kahil the shoemaker. On November 29, 1947, he purchased the remaining scrolls, one of which was a scroll of the prophet Isaiah. Coincidentally, November 29, 1947, is the day the United Nations voted to partition Palestine and allow Israel statehood. On the same day, the ancient prophecies of Isaiah and the ancient land of Israel were returned to Jewish hands. These two seemingly unrelated events have launched a revolution in the way we understand our faith and the way we understand the Bible.

The Jewish return to the land of Israel and the reestablishment of a Jewish state came as a fulfillment of biblical prophecy. After those two events, it was no longer possible for Christians to dismiss the Jewish people. The ancient prophecies concerning Israel were coming true. Christian thinkers and theologians needed to reconsider the Israel question.

THE MODERN JEWISH ROOTS MOVEMENT

The modern-day Jewish Roots movement is born out of an intersection of these things. The Holocaust, the formation of the State of Israel and the discovery of the Dead Sea Scrolls all combined to spark a complete renaissance in the way that early Christianity is studied and understood. Through the work of Jewish Roots scholars, we are now able to read and understand the Gospel from its Jewish context for the first time since the days of the Apostles. The followers of Yeshua are returning to the ways of Torah. Believers are uncovering the original shape and form of the faith. It is a prophetic reawakening, coinciding with the return of the Jewish people to their ancient homeland.

The long exile of the Jewish people is at its end. In the same way, the long exile of the Gospel is at an end. Just as the Jewish people are returning to their native soil, we are returning the Gospel to its original matrix of the Torah of Moses.

More than three thousand years ago, Moses foresaw the time of restoration. "And you shall again obey the Lord, and observe all His commandments which I command you today." (Deuteronomy 30:8)

3

WHAT IS THE TORAH?

The Torah is the Law of Moses. Specifically, it is the books of Genesis, Exodus, Leviticus, Numbers and Deuteronomy. This is the 'Law' that Paul often spoke of in his epistles. Paul used the Greek word *nomos* to translate the Hebrew word *torah*. The word *nomos* means "law," but the Torah is more than just law. It is more than just a legal code.

Paul wrote in Greek, but the concepts he was communicating were Hebrew. They were concepts taken from the Hebrew Scriptures and the Hebrew religion. Although the Greek word *nomos* means "law," its Hebrew equivalent, *torah*, is considerably broader.

BOWS AND ARROWS

Torah comes from a Hebrew root word that is used as an archery term meaning "to take aim, to shoot," such as shooting an arrow in order to hit a target. It is derived from the Hebrew verb *yarah*, "to cast, throw, shoot." The essence of this word then is "to hit the mark." The Torah is God's aim for us.

The opposite of *torah* is *chata*, which means "to miss the mark." *Chata* is the word translated as "sin" in our Bibles. Paul tells us that all have sinned and fallen short of the mark.[14] Do you see the picture? The Torah is the target for which we aim our arrow. When our shot misses and falls short of the target, we have sinned. Sin is missing the mark of the Torah.

My sons and I recently took up archery. We purchased three bows and a few quivers full of arrows and set to work puncturing an old crib mattress that we set up as a target in our backyard. After launching several volleys of arrows, I realized that I am a terrible 'sinner.' Shot after shot completely missed the target. If the definition of sin is to be understood as "missing the mark," then, in terms of archery, I am hopelessly sinful indeed!

After I buried several arrows into the planks of our next-door neighbor's wooden fence, my wife forbade me from shooting in the backyard. Like Paul in his epistle to Timothy, I can claim to be among the worst of sinners, in regard to archery and in regard to Torah. In archery I can't even hit the target, much less a bull's-eye. In regard to Torah I have a heart prone toward sin. I am a mark-misser.

Torah is the mark for which we are to aim. It is God's standard of righteousness. Sin is our failure to hit that mark. And we all fail to hit the mark. "The law [Torah] of the Lord is perfect" (Psalm 19:7), but we are not. "All have sinned and fall short of the glory of God." (Romans 3:23) The Apostle John described it in no uncertain terms: "Everyone who practices sin also practices lawlessness [Torahlessness]; and sin is lawlessness." (1 John 3:4) Sin, properly defined, is transgression of Torah. We all miss the target. We all sin.

THE END OF THE TORAH

There is a point at which the Torah aims. The bull's-eye of Torah, the careful aim of Torah (*yarah*) is the perfect Messiah. This is why Paul wrote in his epistle to the Romans, "Messiah is the end of the law [Torah]." (Romans 10:4)

Unfortunately, traditional Christian interpretation misunderstood Paul's words to mean that Messiah is the cancellation of the Torah. The Greek of Romans 10:4 is best understood to mean that Messiah is the "goal" of the Torah. The Greek word *telos*, which is translated as "end," is the same word we use in English words like telephone, television and telescope. *Telos* implies arrival at a goal. The sound of one's voice on the telephone arrives at the goal of the telephone on the other end. That reading fits the context of Romans 10:4 as well. Messiah is the destination at which the journey of Torah arrives.

Yet, there is an end for which the Torah reaches. Paul writes, "Messiah is the end of the Torah," and again in his epistle to the Galatians he writes, "The law [Torah] has become our tutor *to lead us* to Messiah." (Galatians 3:24) In this sense, Messiah is the goal of the Torah. Is Messiah to be understood as the ending of the Torah then? No. He is the end, but not the ending. He is the goal of the Torah, but not the termination of it. In fact, He Himself said, "Do not think that I came to abolish the law [Torah]." (Matthew 5:17)

THE INSTRUCTIONS

The Hebrew archery term *yarah* is also used to mean "teaching." Torah in many contexts means instruction and teaching. Torah is the impartation of God's direction, instruction, teaching and guidance. It is like God's instruction manual for life.

Several years ago I purchased a VCR with a built-in digital clock and timer. I plugged in the VCR and started to use it, but I never knew how to program it. I could not use it to its fullest potential because I did not know how to set the clock or program the timer. Instead I left the clock endlessly blinking. "12:00...12:00...12:00... 12:00." One day I finally dug out the instructions that came with the VCR and learned how to program it.

A short time later we bought a DVD player to replace the VCR. According to the DVD player, the time is still 12:00.

When God made human beings, He made an instruction manual to accompany them. It is called the "Torah." We do not function to our fullest potential without the instructions. The Ten Commandments, for example, are one part of the instruction manual for human life.

ALL SCRIPTURE IS TORAH

When we speak of the Law (or Torah), we immediately think in terms of Genesis, Exodus, Leviticus, Numbers and Deuteronomy. Those are the books of Moses. But Torah is not limited to the five books of Moses. As we learned above, Torah does not just mean "law," it also means "teaching." Genesis, Exodus, Leviticus, Numbers and Deuteronomy are the teaching of Moses, the Torah of Moses. But in a broader sense, all of Scripture is God-breathed. Therefore, when the rabbis spoke of the Torah, they generally included all of the Scriptures in the term. The Psalms and the Prophets, and even the little scrolls of Esther and the book of Ruth, are all considered parts of the Torah of Israel. That is why Paul sometimes said, "It is written in the Law," and then quoted from Psalms.[15] The Master Himself did the same thing.[16] In one sense, the entire Old Testament is Torah.

For believers in Yeshua, the Torah is broader yet. The Gospels, Paul's writings and epistles and the Revelation of John are also Torah. The entire Bible is God's teaching built upon the Torah of Moses.

In classical Judaism, even the rabbis' extended teachings came to be termed "Torah." The oral traditions, customs and law, including the *Talmud* and other later writings, are regarded as additional members of the extended family of Torah.[17] They all teach, in one form or another, and they are all based upon the five books of Moses.

For the purposes of this book, when I speak of the Torah, I am speaking of the formal Torah in its narrowest sense—the five books of Moses: specifically Genesis, Exodus, Leviticus, Numbers and Deuteronomy.

The Torah Is Not the Old Covenant

The Torah is covenantal. A covenant is a contract specifying terms and conditions incumbent upon both parties. It is a list of obligations. But more than a simple agreement, a covenant is the defining of a relationship between two parties. Technically, Torah is not one single covenant. It contains several different covenants. Paul refers to the covenants in the Torah as the "covenants of promise."[18] The Torah contains the covenant God made with Noah.[19] It contains the covenants He made with Abraham, Isaac and Jacob. It contains the covenant He made with Israel at Mount Sinai. It contains the covenant He made with the house of Aaron[20] and the descendents of Phinehas the priest.[21] It contains the covenant Moses made with Israel by the Jordan River, and it contains a definition of the 'new covenant' in Jeremiah 31. Therefore, it is not quite correct to think of the Torah as the 'old covenant.' Rather it is many covenants. On the other hand, it is fair (though not entirely accurate) to consider the laws of Torah as a covenant because at Mount Sinai, Israel made a covenant with God by which she agreed to keep His laws.[22] Therefore, the Torah is referred to as the book of the covenant,[23] but it is not referred to as the old covenant except in one sense.

The covenant God made with Israel at Mount Sinai is a legally binding agreement between God and His people Israel. In 2 Corinthians 3:14 Paul referred to the Torah of Moses as the old covenant so long as it was read without the realization of Messiah. He said that once we are in Messiah, the veil is "removed." The Torah remains, but the veil concealing Messiah within it is removed. Similarly, the book of Hebrews quotes the prophet Jeremiah to prove that in the new covenant, the Torah is written upon our hearts.

> For this is the covenant that I will make with the house of Israel after those days, says the Lord: I will put My laws [Torah] into their minds, and I will write them on their hearts. (Hebrews 8:10 quoting Jeremiah 31:33)

It is not quite correct to equate the Torah and the old covenant because there is Torah in the new covenant too. Nevertheless, it is correct to think of the Torah as God's covenant with Israel. According to Jeremiah, Paul and the writer of Hebrews, the newness or oldness of the covenant depends on where one stands in regard to Messiah.

◊ Old Covenant: The attempt to keep the Torah according to the covenant at Sinai without realization of Messiah, resulting in condemnation.

◊ New Covenant: The writing of the Torah on our hearts through the realization of Messiah according to the covenant in Jeremiah 31, resulting in salvation.

If that seems confusing, don't worry about it now. We will take a closer look at the new covenant in later chapters.

THE WEDDING VOWS

Covenants are not something we generally encounter in the modern world. One form of covenant that is still with us today, however, is the marriage covenant. The Torah is like a marriage covenant between God and Israel.

Their romance actually began while Israel was still in Egypt. There the Lord declared to Israel, "I will take you for My people, and I will be your God." (Exodus 6:7) This expression is close to an ancient legal formulation from the sphere of marriage. In ancient Near East marriages, the groom declared, "You will be my wife and I will be your husband."[24] In a sense, it is as if God had declared His intention to marry the people of Israel.

The people of Israel are the object of God's affection. At Mount Sinai, He was like the suitor, asking for her hand in marriage. He was to be their God; they were to be His people.

The giving of the law at Mount Sinai is described in Jewish literature as a betrothal and a wedding. In Jewish tradition, one's wedding vows are written out in a formal legal document called a *ketubah*. It is a contract containing all the terms and conditions incumbent upon the bride and groom. The responsibilities of both parties are spelled out clearly. It is a covenant document. Typically, the married couple displays this wedding contract prominently in their home as a piece of artwork celebrating their union. Even in modern Western weddings, the repeating of vows retains vestiges of these nuptial contracts.

The rabbis compared the Torah to a *ketubah*.[25] Where God is likened unto the groom, Israel is likened unto the bride and the Torah is likened unto the *ketubah* that spells out the terms and conditions of their marriage. The Ten Commandments form the summary of their marital statement. Treasured like the *ketubah* in the married couple's home, the tablets of the Ten Commandments were kept inside the Ark at the center of the Tabernacle.

LEGALISM VS. OBEDIENCE

The Torah was not given as a means to attain salvation. The idea that one must, or even can, merit salvation through works is legalism. The Torah gives us a picture of salvation and redemption. It shows us that when God gave Israel the Torah at Mount Sinai, they were already a redeemed people.

In the most ancient reckoning of the Ten Commandments, the first commandment is not the prohibition on idolatry; it is a simple acknowledgement that God exists. In Exodus 20:2, the Lord declares, "I am the Lord your God who brought you out of the land of Egypt, out of the house of slavery." In the days of the Apostles, this simple statement was regarded as the first of the Ten Commandments.

Redemption must precede commandments. The salvation of Israel from Egypt is a physical dramatization of our own salvation from sin and death. In the story of the Exodus, we learn that before we can receive the Torah, we must already be 'saved.'

Israel's salvation from Egypt was not accorded to her on the basis of her obedience to the commandments. She was already redeemed (on no merit of her own) before the laws at Sinai were given to her. Thus the first declaration is a reminder of their redeemed status. Only because they were already saved were they able to receive God's commands.

True legalism continually attempts to reverse this process by claiming that one's obedience to certain commandments (or all the commandments) is the mechanism by which salvation is earned. The first of the Ten Commandments directly contradicts this notion. Salvation and relationship with God precede the Torah.

Oftentimes, believers avoid Torah because they are afraid of falling into legalism. But obedience is not legalism. If keeping the Torah were necessary for salvation, we would all fail because "all have sinned and fall short of the glory of God." (Romans 3:23) The Torah was never meant to be the means by which a person could earn His salvation. Legalism says, "I must obey God in order to be saved." Grace says, "I must obey because I am saved."

So what is the Torah? The Law, a target, the aim, the instruction of God, God's teaching, the five books of Moses, the whole of Scripture, a covenant, both the old covenant and the new covenant, a *ketubah*... There must be a shorter explanation! Actually, the Torah can be summed up in just a few words. In the next chapter, we will read a story drawn from Jewish literature about summing up the Torah.

4

Summing Up the Torah

The Man Who Stood on One Foot

When Yeshua was a little boy and not yet known to the world, a certain Gentile who had lost faith in idols decided it would be better to worship the God of Israel. But there was one small problem. The problem was what the Jews called their Torah: the Law.

"I want to know this God now," the man complained, "I don't have time to learn the whole Law." He thought about it for a while and came up with a plan. "I will go to the greatest Sages and Torah teachers and have them teach me a short version of the Law."

Now, in those days, the two greatest teachers of the Torah were the great sage Rabbi Hillel and his colleague Rabbi Shammai. Shammai was known for being a very strict teacher. Hillel was known for being somewhat gentler.

The Gentile went first to Rabbi Shammai. Rabbi Shammai had a long measuring stick called a builder's cubit in his hand. The Gentile said to him, "Rabbi Shammai, teach me the whole Torah, but do it while I stand on one foot."

Now, standing on one foot is easy to do for a short while, but after a few minutes, you start to lose your balance. What the Gentile meant was, "Teach me the whole Torah, but do it quickly. No longer than just a minute or two!" He proceeded to stand on one foot.

Rabbi Shammai could not believe his ears (or his eyes for that matter). "Who does this Gentile think he is? Teach the whole Torah while he stands on one foot? The whole Torah of Moses?" Shammai took his builder's cubit, whacked the tottering Gentile, and drove him away.

The Gentile thought, "Oh well, I'll try again." He went to Rabbi Hillel and said, "Teach me the whole Torah while I stand on one foot."

Without hesitation, Rabbi Hillel said, "What is hateful to you, do not do to your neighbor. That is the whole Torah. The rest is the commentary on it. Now go and study the rest."

The Gentile was still standing on one foot, but Rabbi Hillel was done. The Gentile went away and began to study.[26]

The Builder's Cubit

Let's take a look at some of the deeper meanings of this story. Why was Rabbi Shammai holding a builder's cubit? Perhaps he was a carpenter. If so, he would not have been the only first-century rabbi to make his living in carpentry. Perhaps the measuring stick is meant to represent the Torah. The Torah can be compared to a builder's cubit.

The basic unit of measure in the biblical world was the cubit. A cubit is the length from the elbow to the tip of the finger. The problem with the cubit is that it is subjective. Everyone's measure of a cubit will be different, depending on the length of one's arm. The average man's arm length will approximate a cubit, but it is too inexact to build with. Imagine two carpenters working on the same building. One has short arms; the other has long arms. Each one builds his side of the building twelve cubits high. What will happen? The structure will be lopsided.

This can be compared to subjective morality. God has given us all an innate sense of right and wrong. A conscience. But it is subjective. What is right or wrong for me might not seem right or wrong for you.

To solve the cubit problem, the ancient world introduced the builder's cubit rod. It was a standardized unit of measure. If a board needed to be twelve cubits long, you could measure that length exactly. You could be confident that your cubit was the same as everyone else's.

The Torah is like the builder's cubit rod. To speak figuratively, it could be compared to the length from God's elbow to the tip of His finger. It is His standard, an objective standard of right and wrong. It is not based on what feels right for me or doesn't feel right for me. It is black and white; it is right and wrong; it is thou shalt and thou shalt not; it is clean and unclean; it is holy and profane. It is a universal standard of righteousness. That's how Rabbi Shammai used it. He used the builder's cubit to beat up the man. He used it to drive him away. He summed up the Torah while the man stood on one foot by giving him a sound bruising.

Whenever we compare ourselves to God's righteous standard, we will experience the same bruising.

Do Unto Others

When the Gentile came to Rabbi Hillel and said, "Teach me the whole Law while I stand on one foot," the rabbi replied, "That which is hateful to you do not do unto others. The rest is commentary; now go and study." Did Rabbi Hillel mean that the other commandments were irrelevant? Did he mean that nothing else in God's Word mattered other than being civil and avoiding injury? Of course not. He was a teacher of the Law. He was not issuing a new law or an improved Word of God. Rather, he was distilling God's Word down to its essence.

One generation later, Yeshua told His disciples, "So in everything, do to others what you would have them do to you, for this sums up the Law and the Prophets." (Matthew 7:12 NIV) Did Yeshua mean that the other commandments were irrelevant? Did He mean that nothing else mattered? Of course not. He also told them, "Whoever then annuls one of the least of these commandments, and teaches others *to do* the same, shall be called least in the kingdom of heaven; but whoever keeps and teaches *them*, he shall be called great in the kingdom of heaven." (Matthew 5:19)

A generation later the famous Rabbi Akiva is quoted as saying the commandment to love one's neighbor as oneself is "the greatest principle in the Torah."[27] Yeshua Himself placed the commandment "Love your neighbor as yourself" second only to "Love the Lord your God with all your heart, and with all your soul, and with all your mind and with all your strength."[28]

Do you see a pattern developing? Rabbi Hillel, Rabbi Yeshua and Rabbi Akiva all taught that the result of Torah, the guiding principal of Torah, the heart and center of Torah, and every true extension of Torah is LOVE.

Let's check with one more rabbi on the topic. After the days of Yeshua, but before the days of Akiva, a rabbi named Paul wrote on this very topic. In Romans 13, Paul said:

> Owe nothing to anyone except to love one another; for he who loves his neighbor has fulfilled *the* law. For this, "You shall not commit adultery, you shall not murder, you shall not steal, you shall not covet," and if there is any other commandment, it is summed up in this saying, "You shall love your neighbor as yourself." Love does no wrong to a neighbor; therefore love is the fulfillment of *the* law [Torah] (Romans 13:8–10)

In Galatians, Paul succinctly stated this premise by saying, "For the whole Law [Torah] is fulfilled in one word, in the *statement*, 'You shall love your neighbor as yourself.'" (Galatians 5:14) But wouldn't it be absurd to take that as a blanket justification for disregarding whatever commandments we don't like on the basis that as long as we love one another, nothing else matters? One might just as effectively suggest, "As long as I love my neighbor, it is all right to eat whatever I want, do whatever I want and sleep with whomever I want." But that would not be demonstrating real love, would it?

So what is real love? The commandments are acts of real love. Love is not the replacement of the Torah; it is the summary of the Torah. Or, as Akiva put it: It is the greatest principle of the Torah.

Love God and love your neighbor. Yeshua said, "On these two commandments hang all the Law and the Prophets." (Matthew 22:40 NKJV) We can compare the Torah and the Prophets to a suit and tie hanging on a clothes-hanger. One does not discard the suit and tie and dress himself in the clothes hanger! Rather, it is the clothes hanger that holds the suit and tie together. It is love, love of God and neighbor, that holds the Torah and the Prophets, with all their commandments, together.

That is why the practice of God's Word must result in love. For example, if I set out to keep a particular commandment but find myself arguing, insulting and embittering others over it, then I may have kept the commandment, but I have failed to keep God's Torah, because the essence of it is love—love of God and love of neighbor.

God's Torah is the equation. The performance of His commandments is the solution. Love is the governing principle by which the solution must be checked for accuracy.

In the Romans 13 passage, Paul stated that any one of the commandments could be summed up in loving our neighbor. This means that every commandment of God's Word is an act of love. Therefore, breaking the commandments is the opposite of love. The opposite of love is not hatred; it is selfishness—love of self.

The commandments teach us to love others as ourselves. Submitting to the commandments displays God's love because those commandments are contrary to our lazy, selfish nature. When we truly keep the commandments, we are loving. And when we truly love God and others, we will keep the commandments.

LOVE MADE COMPLETE

How ironic that we might take the words of Paul and Yeshua, who tell us the commandments are summarized in love, and use those words as a justification for breaking the commandments. "I don't need the letter of the law because I am under the law of love." When Paul indicated that the entire Torah could be summed up in a single command, he was joining his voice to the voice of Yeshua and to the voices of the most famous rabbis of Judaism. Love is a summary of the commandments, and the commandments are all acts of love.

> The one who says, "I have come to know Him," and does not keep His commandments, is a liar, and the truth is not in him; but whoever keeps His word, in him the love of God has truly been perfected. (1 John 2:4–5)

We must protect the biblical concept of love from being so generalized that it loses all meaning. Love is to be the preeminent virtue practiced by believers. The Torah is summed up in love; not by rendering all other requirements inconsequential, but in that love is fundamental to all of the Torah's other requirements and ultimately leads to the observance of all the others.

The '60s concept where love is seen as its own law and the Christian heart provides its own standards is a hippy delusion without scriptural warrant.

THE WOMAN CAUGHT IN ADULTERY

The famous story in John 8 tells of a time when the scribes and the Pharisees brought a woman caught in adultery before Yeshua. At the end of the story, Yeshua told the adulterous woman, "I do not condemn you." (John 8:11) He sent her away free of punishment—obviously a loving thing to do. But if the Torah really demands that a person caught committing adultery should be stoned (and it does), then Yeshua broke the Torah by letting her go, didn't He?

But wait! If Yeshua broke the Torah, then He sinned by letting her go. After all, sin is transgression of the Torah.[29] And if He sinned, then He cannot be the sinless Redeemer. This story needs a closer look!

THE NEW LAW OF LOVE?

Some teach that Yeshua set aside the old law of punishment and wrath in favor of a new law of love and mercy. Under the old law, the woman would have been stoned. Under the new law of love, she is absolved. But Yeshua told us that we must never think that He came to do away with the Torah of Moses. He doesn't allow that kind of thinking. Something else is going on in the story.

The gospel writer tells us the religious officials were using the question as a trap, in order to have a basis for accusing Yeshua. "Now in the Law [Torah] Moses commanded us to stone such women; what then do You say?" (John 8:5)

The trap is very clever, similar to the question about paying taxes to Caesar. No matter how He might answer, they would have grounds to form an accusation against him. If Yeshua said, "Stone her," they could accuse Him before the Romans because the Romans had taken away the power of corporal punishment from the Sanhedrin.[30] The Jewish court no longer had legal authority to stone anyone. (Incidentally, that is why they needed Pilate to execute Yeshua, as it says in John 18:31, "We are not permitted to put anyone to death.")

On the other hand, if He said, "Show some love and let her go," they could accuse Him of advocating lawlessness. "This man teaches against the Torah of Moses," they could have claimed, "He sanctions adultery."

The ancient Sages of Judaism recognized that God's strict Word must be mitigated by God's love and mercy whenever possible. Just as God always had mercy on Israel, so too love must be shown to others. After all, the Torah says, "Love your neighbor as yourself." (Leviticus 19:18) For that reason, the Sages of the Sanhedrin would normally try to avoid issuing a death sentence. One ancient Jewish source says, "A Sanhedrin which executed a person once in seven years was called murderous."[31] However, the Judges of Israel were bound to keep the letter of the law. They could not arbitrarily set aside the Word of God on the basis that they felt compassion or pity for the accused. So what did they do? How did they show love while still keeping the law? Being good lawyers, they used legal loopholes.

LEGAL LOOPHOLES

In most cases, the legal loophole they used was the disqualification of the witnesses. The Torah says that every allegation must be established by two eyewitnesses.[32] If there were no eyewitnesses, then the case had to be dropped, even if the person's guilt was obvious. Oftentimes, witnesses were disqualified before the trial even began "unless the person was known to lead a reputable life and be utterly disinterested."[33] A relative of the accused, an enemy of the accused or anyone with a shady reputation was automatically disqualified. Their testimony could not be considered reliable.

Without reliable eyewitnesses, God's Word did not allow a trial or punishment to take place.

Even if the case went to court, the judges were expected to attempt to disqualify the testimony of the witnesses through vigorous cross-examination. In a popular legend similar to the story in John 8, the prophet Daniel was called upon to preside over a trial where a woman was falsely accused of adultery.[34] Through cross-examination, he disqualified the witnesses and the woman went free.

Yeshua employed a similar approach. Rather than try to defend the woman (who really was guilty) or bend the law (which does not bend), He disqualified the witnesses. He did it through what appears to be supernatural means. He said, "He who is without sin among you, let him *be the* first to throw a stone at her." (John 8:7) According to the Torah, only qualified eyewitnesses could cast the first stones. Each man present was supernaturally conscience stricken. "When they heard it, they *began* to go out one by one, beginning with the older ones, and He was left alone, and the woman, where she was, in the center *of the court*." (John 8:9)

Without witnesses, there is no trial. Without witnesses, the Torah says that the woman must go free. Yeshua asked her, "Woman, where are they? Did no one condemn you?" (John 8:10)

Through a legal technicality, He freed her from the punishment of the Torah. The important thing to realize, though, is that He did it within the boundaries of the Torah. Like the Sages and Torah-lawyers of His day, He was able to avert the death penalty by disqualifying the witnesses. The only difference is that Yeshua did it without investigation or cross-examination. He let each man's own heart and conscience condemn him.

Contrary to the opinion that this story shows how Yeshua disregarded the Torah in favor of a new order of love and grace, the story actually shows how He used Torah commandments to save the woman. The Torah says there must be two witnesses. By the time Yeshua was done writing in the dust, there were no witnesses left. The woman was saved by the Torah.

By disqualifying the witnesses and releasing the woman, Yeshua escaped the religious leaders' clever trap. However, His compassion for the woman was genuine. When He sent her away, He told her, "I do not condemn you, either. Go. From now on sin no more." (John 8:11) He used the Torah to save her and then placed the Torah of His love before her as a pathway to turn her life to the Father. "From now on sin no more."

Yeshua Himself is not above the Torah of God, for it is His own law. Yeshua is God's Word made flesh; how then could He be against God's Word? If He could have dismissed the Torah's requirement with a wave of his hand, there would have been no need for Him to suffer and die. God could have chosen to have arbitrary mercy upon us.

Instead, in order to save us, He employed another technical loophole in the Torah. By taking on the full measure of the Torah's punishment, Yeshua used the Torah, and the rules of the Torah, to save us. By satisfying the demands of the Torah with His own righteous life and innocent death, He sets us free from condemnation. Like the woman in the story, He sets us free from condemnation and then, like the woman in the story, tells us, "I do not condemn you, either. Go. From now on sin no more."

That is the Law of Love.

While Standing on One Foot

When the Gentile came to Rabbi Shammai and said, "Teach me the whole Torah while I stand on one foot," the rabbi replied by smacking him with the builder's cubit. The Torah with its commands is the builder's cubit; it is God's standard of righteousness. It is that by which we must measure ourselves. But if the Torah can be compared to the length from God's elbow to the tip of His finger (as it were), we must also understand that God's arm is the measure of Torah, and God's arm is the arm of love. Thus the measure of Torah is love. Hence the wisdom of Rabbi Hillel's answer. The outcome of Torah—the ultimate result—is a measure of love.

We all fall short of the standard of righteousness, which is Torah. The builder's cubit of Torah smacks all of us. Yet the outcome is love, as it says:

> For God so loved the world, that He gave His only begotten Son, that whoever believes in Him shall not perish, but have eternal life. For God did not send the Son into the world to judge the world, but that the world might be saved through Him. (John 3:16–17)

The love that brought the incarnation, the crucifixion and the resurrection is the same love that gave the Torah. The exodus from Egypt, the voice at Sinai, the Ten Commandments, the books of Moses, and the covenants with Abraham, Isaac and Jacob—these were acts of love.

Now, let's go and study.

5

TORAH AND
THE NEW TESTAMENT

> And He came to Nazareth, where He had been brought
> up; and as was His custom, He entered the synagogue on
> the Sabbath, and stood up to read. (Luke 4:16)

Sometime near the outset of His ministry, Yeshua returned to
His hometown, the village of Nazareth. On the Sabbath, He
attended the synagogue. Luke points out that this was His custom,
which is to say, He never missed Sabbath services.

THE BIBLE JESUS READ

We are uncertain of exactly how a first-century Galilean synagogue
Sabbath service was conducted. Luke chapter four is the oldest
existing description of a Jewish synagogue service, and the details
there are sparse. Nevertheless, most of the conventions one might
find in any modern Sabbath synagogue service seem to have been
present. Luke tells us there was teaching in the synagogue, the
Torah was read aloud and a section from the Prophets was also
read aloud. Things have not changed much since then.

Luke tells us He "stood up to read." From a non-Jewish perspective we would understand that phrase to be directly connected
with the following verse: That is, He stood up to read from the
scroll of the prophet Isaiah. From a Jewish perspective, however,
the words "stood up to read" clearly imply that He stood to read
Torah. Even in modern synagogues, the reader called up to read

from the prophets must first read the last few verses of that week's Torah portion. That Yeshua goes on to read from the scroll of the prophet Isaiah indicates that Yeshua was the last reader called to read the Torah that Sabbath.

It might have happened like this. A synagogue official opened the ark in which the scrolls were kept and removed the scroll of the Torah from it. In a solemn procession, he placed it on the platform from which it would be read. The cantor or the synagogue attendant, depending on the local custom, opened the scroll to the appropriate reading for the day. It may have been wound to somewhere in Deuteronomy, which pairs with readings from Isaiah in today's annual cycle. The synagogue official called seven readers to read the Torah on the Sabbath.[35] The first reader to be called up, as always, was a priest; that is, someone descended from Moses' brother Aaron. The second reader to be called up was always a Levite. The remaining readers could be any Jew in the community.

As the guest of honor that Sabbath, Yeshua was not called to read until six readers had stood to read before Him. The place of seventh reader is a special honor because the seventh reader also does the reading from the prophets.[36]

After the sixth reader had sat down, the cantor called out across the congregation, "Approach, Yeshua. Arise, Yeshua ben Yosef." Luke tells us He then "stood up to read." (Luke 4:16)

After He finished reading the appropriate portion from the scroll of the Torah, the Torah was rolled back up and set aside. The synagogue official then removed the scroll of the prophets and handed it to Yeshua. Luke tells us that Yeshua opened the scroll of Isaiah and found the place from which He would read.

After completing the reading, He rolled the scroll of Isaiah back up and sat down. This does not mean that he returned to His seat in the congregation, but that He sat down to teach. Among the early Sages, teachers sat to deliver their discourses. For Luke to tell us that He "sat down" (Luke 4:20) would be the equivalent in modern conventions of telling us that He stepped up to the pulpit. Everyone's eyes were riveted on Him because He was to deliver the teaching that day—and He did. He taught from the Old Testament. After all, the Old Testament was the Bible Jesus read.

In his book *The Bible Jesus Read*, best-selling author Phillip Yancey observes that Yeshua did not have a New Testament in His Bible. The New Testament had not yet been written. But neither did His Bible have an Old Testament. No one thought of God's eternal Word as an 'Old Testament.' In the days of Yeshua, the Old Testament was simply called the Scriptures.

Today, some Bibles are printed without the Old Testament. They begin at the Gospel of Matthew. Even when our Bibles do contain the Old Testament Scriptures, they are not always read. Those books are typically regarded as a very long introduction to Matthew. Though Christians study it in Sunday school and enjoy reading its stories, few regard the Old Testament as relevant for how to live life.

How sad to think that the followers of Yeshua today rarely read the Bible He read. We have surprisingly little interest in the Scriptures that shaped His life and teaching. We regard the Bible of Yeshua as irrelevant. But is it really?

Yeshua didn't think so. He said that those Scriptures testified about Him.[37] He quoted them in order to correct and rebuke people. He interpreted them to give His disciples guidance. He quoted verses from Deuteronomy to defeat the devil in head-to-head spiritual warfare. His first recorded words after His baptism are quotations from the Torah of Moses[38] and His last utterance from the cross was a quotation from the Psalms of David.[39]

Yeshua spent the day of His resurrection discussing those old Scriptures with His disciples. He showed them the things written about Him "in the Law [Torah] of Moses and the Prophets and the Psalms."[40] There is certainly a lot of 'Old Testament' in the New Testament.

The Bible itself refers to neither the Hebrew Scriptures (the ones we call 'old') nor the Apostolic Scriptures (the ones we call 'new') as old or new. Those are titles that man has created. If anything, we should be amazed at how the Hebrew Scriptures and the Apostolic Scriptures are seamlessly intertwined.

Paul once wrote to his student Timothy, saying, "All Scripture is inspired by God and profitable for teaching, for reproof, for correction, for training in righteousness; so that the man of God may be adequate, equipped for every good work." (2 Timothy 3:16–17) But Timothy did not have a New Testament; his Bible was the Hebrew

Scriptures. Could Paul really have expected believers to be taught, rebuked, corrected, trained and equipped for good works from the Old Testament? Apparently so.

Yeshua and Paul and all the 'New Testament' writers regarded the Hebrew Scriptures—particularly the five books of Moses—as the bedrock foundation on which they built their teaching. To them, those books were the only Scriptures. Paul did not know that his epistles would one day be collected as Scripture. He did not imagine himself writing new books of the Bible. He did not even live long enough to see the written Gospels produced. As far as Paul knew, the Hebrew Scriptures were the only Scriptures.

How odd for us to imagine that those Scriptures are not relevant to believers today. They were certainly relevant to Yeshua and Paul. Not only did they use them for teaching, rebuking, correcting and training in righteousness, they lived their lives by them. Near the end of his life Paul declared himself fully obedient to the Torah of Moses.[41] Yeshua, of course, never broke a commandment of the Torah.[42] As followers of Yeshua and students of Paul, perhaps we should emulate them.

In his book *Yeshua: A Guide to the Real Jesus and the Original Church*, Dr. Ron Moseley wryly observes, "Since the first century, the church, for the most part, has misunderstood the law, which both Jesus and Paul dearly loved and by which they both lived." He goes on to say, "Jesus' purpose was to establish God's Torah among the Jews. Paul's purpose was to extend forth God's Torah to embrace the non-Jews. For both Jesus and Paul, Torah was grace."[43] The prophet Isaiah tells us that Messiah was sent to bring the Torah even to the uttermost parts of the earth.[44]

In fact, we should probably consider using the term "Hebrew Scriptures" to describe the Old Testament. While they certainly are old, they contain the eternal, living words of God. They contain scrolls first committed to writing some 3,400 years ago. But they are not old in the sense of obsolete. They are "living oracles."[45] They reveal the person of Messiah.[46] They contain the glory of the new covenant.[47] They are the standard of righteousness for which we are to train. They equip us to perform the good deeds we are called to do.[48] They comprise the Bible Jesus read.

The Parts of the Bible

A foolish man set out to build a house. He wondered where to begin. "Should I build the front door first?" he wondered. "Perhaps I should start with the kitchen, or maybe the master bedroom. Better yet, I should build the roof first so I don't get rained on while working."

Silly fellow! Everyone knows that to build a solid structure, a builder must start with a foundation. After the foundation is laid, the first floor of the house can be built upon it. The second floor can be added to the first. The roof, which rests over the structure, is built last. Common sense, right? Yet for some reason, we often fail to apply such simple common sense to the interpretation of Scripture. We tend to want to start by building the second floor and the roof.

Just as a house is comprised of different parts, the Bible is comprised of different types of books. The Hebrew Scriptures contain the Torah, the Prophets and the Writings.

As we have already learned, the Torah is the five books of Moses. The Prophets include the oracles of the Prophets and the books of Samuel and Kings. The Writings are the works of poetry, including Psalms and Proverbs and short narratives like Ruth and Ezra. Yeshua Himself referenced this threefold division of the Scriptures.[49]

Similarly, the Apostolic Scriptures (New Testament) are comprised of several parts. They include the Gospels, the Epistles and the Revelation. All of the Scriptures work together to form the whole structure, but they each have a different function.

The Scriptures

Hebrew Scriptures (OT)	Apostolic Scriptures (NT)
Torah	Gospels and Acts
Prophets	The Epistles
Writings	The Revelation

Backward and Upside down

We often spend most of our Bible study time reading and teaching from the Pauline epistles. We also study the Gospels and Revelation. Beyond those, we dabble in the Psalms and Writings, occasionally consult the Prophets, and once in a while glance at the Torah. Our priority of Scripture has the Epistles first and the Torah last. We have arrived at this backward because we have been led to believe that Paul (the writer of the Epistles) taught against Torah, and Yeshua (in the Gospels) did away with Torah. Therefore we regard the Torah and Old Testament as less relevant and authoritative than our New Testament books. But this is backward and upside down. It is like building the second floor of the house before laying a foundation or building the first floor. It is the wrong priority of Scripture.

The correct priority of Scripture is sequential. We should start at the beginning. Paul tells us that a later covenant cannot contradict an earlier covenant.[50] Neither can a later scripture contradict an earlier one. If there were such a contradiction, it would mean that one of the scriptures was wrong (in which case it isn't Holy scripture) or that God had changed His mind (in which case He is inconsistent and fallible). The correct priority of Scripture starts with the Torah.

THE PRIORITY OF SCRIPTURE

The Torah can be likened to the foundation of a house because it is the initial revelation of God. When God spoke the Torah through Moses, it was His introduction of Himself to Israel and the entire world. In the books of Moses, God made His debut. Through the stories and laws of the Torah, we are introduced to who God is, what He is like, how He made the world, why He chose His people, how He redeemed them and what He expects from them. It is a record of God's covenants with His people, and it contains the stipulations of those covenants. Therefore the Torah comes first. Any subsequent revelations, prophecies or scriptures would have to be checked against the Torah for authentication. Any prophet who uttered a prophecy contrary to the Torah was to be regarded as a false prophet.[51] A false prophet's writings would not have been regarded as Scripture.

The writings of the Prophets are built upon the foundation of Torah. They presuppose the authority of the Torah and continually point back toward it. The consistent message of Israel's Prophets was a call to repent and turn back to the covenant norms expressed in the Torah. "Repent because you have broken the Torah," the Prophets said.[52] The Prophets also looked forward to the Kingdom of Heaven on earth when God's Torah would be universally obeyed.[53]

The Writings are also built upon the foundation of Torah. Books like Proverbs continually exhort us to turn to the Torah.[54] The Psalms praise God's Torah and urge us to keep His laws.[55] Ezra tells the story of how the nation was restored to Torah. Any Israelite book that in some way contradicted the Torah would not have been regarded as Scripture. Consistency with the Torah is the litmus test of scriptural authenticity.

The Apostolic Scriptures are also built on the same foundation. Throughout the Gospels, Yeshua proclaimed a message of repentance.[56] He called His people back to the simple truth of Torah[57] and offered His life as a payment for transgressions against the Torah. To validate His teaching, He continually quoted the Hebrew Scriptures.[58] He forbade His disciples from imagining that He might do away with the Torah and even encouraged them to keep the smallest of commandments.[59]

The Epistles are an extension of Yeshua's teaching, but they rest on the foundation of Torah. They are solidly Torah-based. Throughout the Epistles, the Apostles rarely quote Yeshua to prove a point or to introduce a new teaching; instead they cited passages from the Hebrew Scriptures and from the Torah. Paul continually spoke of the Torah, citing passage after passage from the Torah and the Hebrew Scriptures to make his case for the Gospel. His source of authority was the Torah.

Even the book of the Revelation is Torah-based. It contains seemingly endless allusions to the Torah and speaks of the triumphant overcomers as those "who keep the commandments of God and hold to the testimony of Yeshua."[60] The Torah contains God's commandments. The testimony of Yeshua is the Gospel. Therefore the Revelation, which alludes to the whole of Scripture while calling us to the commandments of God and the testimony of Yeshua, is like the roof covering the entire structure.

Yeshua quoted and cited the Torah to make His arguments and prove His identity. Paul also quoted and cited the Torah to make his arguments and prove Yeshua's identity. It would be illogical, then, to suppose that Yeshua and Paul, in the next breath, denied the Torah's authority. According to God's own criteria, any prophet who might contradict His Torah is a false prophet.[61] Therefore, if we find a passage in the Apostolic Scriptures that appears to contradict an earlier revelation of Scripture, then we are misunderstanding the passage. This is not to say that one scripture is more important than another. It does not mean that Torah is more important than the Gospels or the Epistles. But it does mean that Torah must be regarded first, because it was given first. The latter writings presuppose our familiarity with it and must be interpreted in light of it. If we read the Torah through the lenses of the New Testament, we are proceeding in the opposite direction. To fully understand God's Word, we must read the Gospels and Epistles through the lens of Torah.

The Prophets, Writings, Gospels and Epistles all base their authority on the Torah of Moses. If we pull the Torah out from under them, they all collapse, and we are left with a hopeless jumble of confusing scriptures that seem to contradict one another.

This explains why many believers find the Bible so hard to understand. It can be compared to beginning a novel in the last chapter. You would not know who the characters are. You would not know the setting or the plot. You would be left trying to piece together the storyline and making all sorts of assumptions that the author never intended. It makes much more sense to start at the beginning of the book.

In the same way, when we start in the Gospels and Epistles, we are learning about Messiah, but we haven't a notion of what a messiah is or what He is about. We are assuming a knowledge of the God of Israel, but we don't know anything about Him or Israel. We are engaged in conversations about laws we never learned. We are talking about sin and forgiveness, but we don't even have a standard definition of what a sin is. All Scripture is God breathed and equally true and relevant,[62] but let's get first things first. Only when we start with the beginning of the book will we fully understand the middle and the ending. Only after we first lay the foundation of a house can we proceed to build the rest of the structure. When the house rests on a solid foundation, it is unshakable.

The bedrock foundation of the Scriptures is the revelation at Mount Sinai.

6

The Giving of the Torah

At Mount Sinai God came down onto the mountain. That moment marked a critical change in faith and religion forever. No longer was it valid to say, "Whatever you believe is true for you." Or, "Well, I think God is like this," or "My god isn't like that," or "My god is such-and-such." At Mount Sinai, theology ceased to be speculation and became the study of revelation. At Mount Sinai, God told us who He is, and that telling is the Torah. The Torah is His message to us human beings, His self-disclosure.

Before the giving of the Torah at Mount Sinai, we human beings had precious little hope of knowing who God was, what He was like, what He was about or what He wanted. We had no way of comprehending the infinite abstraction of His blessed eternal self. How could we have known the unknowable? We could not have, and we did not.

So we imagined God within our own minds. We saw the sun and imagined a sun god. We saw the moon and imagined a moon god. Theology was speculation at best and superstition at worst.

You might object and say, "Surely Adam and Eve and Noah and the Patriarchs and all those godly men in the book of Genesis knew God before the giving of the Torah at Mount Sinai." Perhaps. How is it then that we know the stories of Adam and Eve and Noah and the Patriarchs? We know about them because their accounts are in the Torah. The book of Genesis is regarded as divine revelation only because of what happened in Exodus 19. If not for the giving of the Torah in Exodus 19, we would not possess the knowledge of God that the Patriarchs possessed.

The Mount Sinai epiphany was not given to one individual. A whole nation heard God speaking. Many people heard the words coming forth from the mountain. Most of the world's major religions trace their faith back to the spiritual endowment of a single individual. Premises of theology, faith and creed are often built upon the subjective experiences of a single person. Not so with Torah. The Torah was given to an entire nation. All the people of Israel heard the voice and saw the fire. It was God's big entrance.

He said, *"Anochi Adonai Eloheicha."* "I am the Lord your God."[63]

It was as if God said, "Hi, I'm God. Allow Me to introduce Myself."

It was an amazing, unparalleled debut onto the scene of human history.

NATURAL LAW

Why did God reveal himself to humanity? Was it simply revelation for the sake of revelation? Was it simply an introduction? "Hi, I'm God. How are you? By the way, I made this place." Perhaps God saw it as a chance to impress us with thunder and lightning. No, God's revelation at Sinai was deliberate. He came down onto the mountain for a reason. He gave the Torah for a purpose. He gave us His laws.

Not that we didn't have any laws prior to Mount Sinai. We had laws. Every human society has laws.

Every society conducts itself under some code of behavior. It may be explicit like the legal codes of Hammurabi, or it may be implicit, like the unwritten laws of hospitality that govern the East. But without a common code of conduct, a society could not be a society. Though ethics vary dramatically from culture to culture, the existence of and need for some kind of ethical system is universally acknowledged. Notions of right and wrong and fair and unfair and honor and dishonor appear to be hardwired into human consciousness. Those primal notions emerge in every human association as some sort of code of behavior. We refer to this impulse toward ethical society as Natural Law.

Natural Law tells us that there is such a thing as wrong and right. It is the primal and universal conscience. We may differ on the specifics of exactly what is wrong and what is right, but as C.S. Lewis pointed out in his apologetics,[64] we all seem to possess a notion that there are right things and wrong things. From where does such a universal notion come? If we are just highly evolved animals, how can we account for this tendency toward moral categories?

The presence of Natural Law in human society is the result of being made in the image of God. We possess a moral conscience. Individually and in association with one another, a pattern of morality emerges because God has made us moral creatures with an instinctual sense of morality. We are intuitively aware of justice and injustice and the need for a system of rules to accommodate justice.

In Romans 2, Paul points out how the tendency toward Natural Law reflects God's Law.[65] He says:

> For when Gentiles who do not have the Law [Torah] do instinctively the things of the Law [Torah], these, not having the Law [Torah], are a law to themselves, in that they show the work of the Law [Torah] written in their hearts, their conscience bearing witness and their thoughts alternately accusing or else defending them. (Romans 2:14–15)

Thus we find within us a reflection of our Creator. Our natural desire for justice and fairness reveals a Maker with similar impulses.

CREATING GOD IN MAN'S IMAGE

By observing a work of art, one can deduce a thing or two about the artist who created it. By observing ourselves, we can deduce a thing or two about God.

Even before Mount Sinai, we were able to conclude that our Creator must have a moral drive similar to our own. If we have a conscience and feelings of right and wrong, this must be something that our Creator possesses.

But Natural Law as expressed in human beings and human societies is deficient. Since the fall of man, we no longer accurately reflect the image of the Creator Who made us. Even the best human efforts to live according to a moral code are flawed. The most moral of human societies are full of injustice and immorality. Human ethics are mutable. Moral absolutes without a higher authority are an impossibility.

While we may have an innate sense of justice, it is a slippery justice that we are willing to apply to others but rarely to ourselves.

From the early beginnings of human religions, the capriciousness of our own behavior had us imagining gods that were just as capricious as we are. We imagined gods motivated by human impulses of selfishness, lust, greed and envy. We imagined the laws governing their behavior to reflect the uncertainty of our own human waywardness.

Thus our absolute moral authorities—i.e., the gods of the ancient world—were hardly in a position to issue moral imperatives. They were as sinful and petty as we are because they were, at best, merely projections of our own selves.

Short of direct revelation from heaven, how else were we to imagine God? If we had to base our assessment of God only on human behavior, God would come out looking very human. We would have to surmise that the Creator possesses the same uncertain and twisted sense of subjective morality that we do, or He must be completely amoral, without connection or concern for human behavior. Both of these versions of God have been imagined at various points in human history. The classical gods of ancient Greece follow the former line of reasoning while Plato's monotheism is built upon the latter. It's not an attractive choice. On the one hand we might have gods who are as ill-tempered and unpredictable as we are, and on the other hand we might have a god who is completely dispassionate.

Fortunately, God did not leave us to speculate. At Mount Sinai, He gave us His laws.

Revelation through Legislation

If I were a god about to reveal myself to my creation for the first time, I would probably compose a nice systematic theology to put into their hands so they could understand me and the universe I had created. I might throw in some convenient math equations to explain the recipe of my godhead. A few diagrams would be useful too.

God doesn't do things like I would.

When God revealed Himself to us, He did not give us a systematic theology, creeds, recipes or diagrams. He gave us a legal code. He gave us laws.

Yet they are more than just laws intended to tidy up human society. They are actual pieces of godliness. Each *mitzvah* (commandment) is a small revelation of God. More than just a rule for governing human behavior, the laws of Torah are a reflection of the Lawgiver.

Yeshua told us that "the mouth speaks out of that which fills the heart." (Matthew 12:34) When God broke the silence and spoke to His creation at Mount Sinai, the words He spoke were the fullness of His heart. Each law, each commandment, no matter how small or seemingly irrelevant, is actually a piece of revelation from God, an overflowing of His heart.

For example, one of the laws given at Mount Sinai is about enemies and donkeys. Exodus 23:5 says, "If you see the donkey of one who hates you lying *helpless* under its load, you shall refrain from leaving it to him; you shall surely release *it* with him."

The law commanding us to assist our enemy when he is in difficulty reveals to us a piece of true godliness. It is a revelation of God that would never have occurred to us naturally. Such a law teaches us about God's mercy and compassion.

Even a moral human being would not feel compelled to help an enemy stand his donkey back up. Your enemy is the person who wants to hurt you and your family. Most of us would rejoice at the sight of our enemy's overturned donkey! We might offer a few encouraging hand gestures, but we certainly would not offer any assistance. Such a commandment is beyond the demands of Natural Law and far beyond the scope of human mercy and compassion. It betrays an origin other than human beings. It is a piece of God.

Comprehending the infinite God is beyond the scope of finite human beings. We could never begin to fathom even a single attribute of God. For example, we do not possess the faculties to wrap our minds around the depth, width and breadth of God's mercy and compassion. We don't have the capacity to understand even that single piece of godliness.

However, we all have enemies, and we all have seen donkeys. Enemies and donkeys are two tangible realities that we can easily comprehend. The Torah conveys to us a piece of godliness through a medium we can understand. When we study the law of helping your enemy stand his donkey back up onto its feet, we have learned a little bit of God's character.

ABOLISHING GOD

Because Torah is both law and revelation, it functions in a dual capacity. On one hand, it is a rule of conduct by which we are held accountable. On the other hand, it is the expression of God in human terms. Torah is more than just legal formulations; it is the revealed person of God dressed in laws and commandments. It is His spoken word written down, His self-disclosure to the world.

When one realizes that Torah is God's self-disclosure to the world, one must also recognize the enormous gravity of declaring parts of that same Torah null or void. Even the smallest commandment of the Torah is suffused with godliness. To declare any commandment as irrelevant or obsolete is to deny the eternal and unchanging nature of God.

As soon as we begin to discard commandments, we have begun editing God. We have started reshaping God into an image we deem more appropriate.

For example, we Westerners find the idea of clean and unclean laws disquieting. It is therefore theologically convenient for us to annul all laws pertaining to clean and unclean. By so doing, we are able to clean up God's image a bit. We feel more comfortable with a God who doesn't make seemingly superstitious distinctions between a menstruating woman and one who is not. But in so doing, we have changed God's self-disclosure to suit our biases. This is a very slippery kind of religion.

When we try to change the Torah or do away with a commandment, it is actually God we are trying to change or do away with.

The Torah is given to us as both law and revelation. As such, when we live our lives according to its commandments, we are living out a revelation of godliness. Outside observers should be able to look at the Torah-observant life and discern in it several truths of godliness. Deuteronomy 4:5–8 says that when Israel lives out the Torah, the world will see God.

Unfortunately, neither Israel nor any other group of people has ever lived out God's Torah in its fullness. Even when the people of Israel have been Torah-observant on the whole, the hearts of men and women are still errant and disobedient. There is considerable disparity between God's Law, our notions of Natural Law, and our behavior. The Torah is the substance of which our deficient Natural Law is only a shadow. There remains a great divorce between God's Law and human beings.

This is why Messiah is necessary. In Messiah, the perfect revelation of godliness is fully realized. Living in complete accordance with God's Law, Messiah is a tangible and intimately knowable representation of the unknowable God. He is the Torah lived out.

One of the purposes of Messiah's redemption is to reconcile the human race to God's Torah. The ultimate completion of His work will be when the Natural Law of human society is identical to the revealed law of Torah. A day is coming when the Torah will be written on the hearts of men and women in vivid detail. Jeremiah 31:33 says, "I will put My law [Torah] within them and on their heart I will write it." This is the very promise of the new covenant.

What does it mean to have the Torah written on our hearts? How is that different from the universal principle of Natural Law? When God's Torah is written on our hearts, there will be no disparity between the Natural Law of humanity and God's revealed Torah. Instead of vague and subjective notions of wrong and right, the Torah of God will be the natural impulse of human morality. In that day, human beings will be accurate reflections of godliness.

Often, however, we labor under the impression that this prophecy has already been completely fulfilled in us. Because we are part of the new covenant (to which Jeremiah was referring) and because we have received the Holy Spirit of God within us, we assume that we must already have God's perfect law placed in our minds and written on our hearts. But is God's Torah really fully written on our hearts?

Many theologians assume that it is. Believers sometimes erroneously suppose that since God's Law is written on their hearts, they should allow their hearts to dictate their behavior. The reasoning goes something like this: "It doesn't feel like keeping the Sabbath is written on my heart. Therefore, this law has been done away with and I need not follow it." But where do we stop with that kind of thinking? One might just as well say, "Since covetousness is written on my heart, the law that says 'Do not covet' has been done away with." In such a theology, our feelings and inclinations are elevated to be the arbiters of truth.

Jeremiah's prophecy of God's Torah being written on the hearts and minds of men and women has not yet been fully realized. Redemption is a process. The Torah is being written on our hearts, but none of us have arrived yet. For this reason, we are still very much in need of Yeshua. He remains the only man to have ever lived life as a perfect expression of God. He remains the only man with the Torah written in full upon His heart. Consequently, we are still very much in need of the written Torah. It remains the only standard we have to measure our errant hearts against.

LITTLE MOUNT SINAIS

Writing the Torah on the hearts of the redeemed is the Holy Spirit's job.[66]

Paul encourages us to rely more and more upon that inner Torah of God's Spirit. In Galatians he reminds us that the acts of the sinful nature are obvious, but against the fruit of the Spirit there is no Torah.[67] The Holy Spirit of God is at work within us as a new Natural Law, and as long as we are in obedience to the Spirit, we are not breaking Torah.

The Spirit will never lead us to break Torah. On the contrary, the Spirit of God is writing Torah onto the hearts of men. As we follow Yeshua and listen to the Spirit of God within us, we are being transformed into living Torahs, living revelations of godliness.

We are like little individual Mount Sinais.

God introduced Himself to the world at Mount Sinai. Through the giving of laws and commandments, He revealed His essential person to humankind. But that revelation is not a static one-time event. Believers are expected to live out those laws and continue to reveal God to the world. We are to be a perpetual Mount Sinai experience to all of creation. In that endeavor, we have had varying degrees of success and failure, but only Messiah has truly accomplished a perfect life of obedience. Now, via the work of His redemption and the transforming power of His indwelling Spirit, we are being conformed to the image of Yeshua. A living copy of the Torah is being written on our hearts. This inner Torah does not negate the written Torah. Instead God's Law is supposed to become a moral reflex for us, a new Natural Law, which enables us to walk in genuine obedience. To the extent that we do so, we are living lives like Messiah, perfect revelations of godliness in human form. This is what it means to be transformed by Messiah.

We can sum it up quite simply. When we see the donkey of someone who hates us fallen down under its load, and we immediately recognize that the right and moral thing to do is to help him stand his donkey back up, and we do it, then we are on the path to godliness.

7

THE INNER TORAH

In the story of Snow White, the wicked queen asks her magic mirror, "Mirror, mirror on the wall, who's the fairest of them all?" The mirror answers, "Snow White is fairest of them all." That was not the answer she wanted.

Many of us have had similarly bad experiences with mirrors. When we ask our bathroom mirrors, "Who is the fairest of them all?" the mirror shows us someone else. It is as if the mirror says, "I don't know who is the fairest, but it sure isn't you." Oh well, looks aren't everything. After all, beauty is only skin deep. A person might have other qualities hidden beneath the surface, right?

THE SOUL MIRROR

But what if you had a spiritual mirror that reflected your inner self? You could call it a 'soul mirror.' Imagine looking into your bathroom mirror, and instead of seeing your perky face, you saw a brutally honest reflection of your soul and all the secret inner things of your heart. Suddenly on display were all the little sins, secret thoughts, pettiness and lusts that are tucked away deep inside. How horrible it would be to find yourself confronted with your own soul, scarred and disfigured by a life of sin. Beauty really is only skin deep! What's under the skin is less than beautiful.

If you had such a mirror, would you want to look into it? Probably not. But James (Yaakov), Yeshua's little brother, tells us that we do have such a mirror. It is the Torah.

> Prove yourselves doers of the word, and not merely hearers who delude themselves. For if anyone is a hearer of

the word and not a doer, he is like a man who looks at his natural face in a mirror; for *once* he has looked at himself and gone away, he has immediately forgotten what kind of person he was. But one who looks intently at the perfect law, the law of liberty, and abides by it, not having become a forgetful hearer but an effectual doer, this man will be blessed in what he does. (James 1:22–25)

James calls the Torah the "perfect law [Torah]," and the "law [Torah] of liberty." I have never looked into a mirror and thought of my reflection as perfect or liberating. Something else is at work here with this marvelous mirror.

Remember, the Torah is a 'soul mirror.' What we see when we look into it is not a reflection of who we are on the outside, but a reflection of who we are on the inside. When a believer looks into the 'soul mirror' of Torah, the reflection he sees staring back at him is not that horrid sin-scarred visage he might expect. It is not his own image at all. It is the reflection of Yeshua. That's how the Torah 'soul mirror' works. As believers, our truest and deepest identity is our new life in Messiah.

Seeing Yeshua in the mirror reminds us that we need to be true to this inner identity. We need to be obedient to the commands of God as the Master, Yeshua, was. Regardless of our own sins, our truest identity is the perfect and liberating reflection of Messiah. Therefore the Torah mirror is the 'perfect Torah' and the 'liberating Torah' because it reflects Messiah within us, and it is Messiah who perfects and liberates.

The Reflection of Messiah

When we turn away from that soul mirror, we risk forgetting the image we saw in the reflection. James says that the person who reads the Torah but does not do what it says is like that person who sees his reflection but then forgets what he or she looks like.

When we look into the Torah, we look into the righteousness of God. It shows us things with which we must deal, commandments to keep, dangers to avoid, and areas in our lives that need to be set right. What we do with that information is up to us.

Our goal should be to remember the face in the mirror. We need to carry that image into our daily lives. Somehow, we must overcome our forgetfulness. We should consciously choose to remember the image in the mirror. It is, after all, who we really are.

For believers, the Torah is not a sterile list of rules. It is a written version of our inner identity—Messiah. We follow it because it is written on our hearts. It defines who we are as new creations.[68]

James urges us to stare intently at our reflection (the image of Messiah) in the Torah, and then go out and practice what we have learned. The man who looks into the Torah but does not do what he learns there is like the man who forgets what he looks like. Only by doing the Word is our inner reality (i.e., Messiah) able to be fully expressed on the outside. James essentially says, "Look in the mirror, then do something about it. Wash your face, comb your hair and brush your teeth. Don't just walk away like a man who forgets what he looks like."

THE KIND OF PEOPLE WE ARE

To the extent that we live out the commands of Torah in our lives, we are living out the righteousness of Messiah. We can pick any commandment from the Torah to see this principle practically applied.

For example, take the commandment to immediately pay the poor man his wages. The Torah says that we must not make needy people wait for their earnings. Instead, we are to compensate them for their work that same day.

> You shall not oppress a hired servant *who* is poor and needy, whether *he is* one of your countrymen or one of your aliens who is in your land in your towns. You shall give him his wages on his day before the sun sets, for he is poor and sets his heart on it; so that he will not cry against you to the Lord and it become sin in you. (Deuteronomy 24:14–15)

When we look into the 'soul mirror' of Torah and come across this commandment, we see the reflection of a generous and considerate person who is quick to help those less fortunate. The face in the mirror is the face of a man (or woman) who does not take advantage of the needy, but goes the extra distance, even inconveniencing himself, to make sure others' daily needs are met. It is the face of a fair employer who treats his employees with dignity and concern. He considers their personal estate before he considers the larger and more pressing concerns of the business.

If, after studying this principal, we return to our lives without implementing the commandment, we are like the man who forgets what he saw in the mirror. If we decide to withhold paying the contractor promptly, or to withhold paying a promised bonus until a more lucrative season, we have forgotten who we really are.

But if, after studying this commandment, we eagerly apply ourselves to treating our employees and dependents with prompt consideration, then we are like the man who remembers what he saw in the mirror. We pay the contractor even before the 30-day deadline because that's the kind of people we are. We pay out the promised bonus because our employees are anticipating it, even though it might make for a financial squeeze.

Consider the commandments of caring for the orphan, widow and stranger, honoring father and mother, showing respect to teachers and elders, not coveting, not stealing and not lying. Consider the implications of more obscure commands such as the one to drive away the mother bird before taking the young or the prohibition on muzzling an ox while it treads out the grain. These are not stern and martial lists of 'thou shalts' and 'thou shalt nots.' They are a reflection of our new identity. The Torah is showing us snapshots of who we really are in Messiah.

But if we hope to enter into the full expression of our new identity in Messiah, we must be doers of God's Word, not just hearers. The Master tells us that a person who hears His words but does not do them is like a man who builds his house on the sand.[69] He is a man without foundation. James tells us that such a man is one who has forgotten what he really looks like. The Torah shows us what we are supposed to look like.

New Creation Theology

When we become believers, we become completely new people. The Bible tells us that we die to our old selves and are raised up as brand new human beings. Even though we are the same people on the outside, a new identity has been imparted to us. In some ways, this identity is legal in nature. After becoming believers, we have been legally adopted into God's family. We are now sons of God. According to Romans 11, we have been grafted into the olive tree of Israel. We are now, according to Ephesians 2, part of the commonwealth of Israel. We have been declared righteous and justified. Our sins have been forgiven. Records of our guilt have been erased. There is no condemnation. These are the legal aspects of our new identity in Messiah.

> Or do you not know that all of us who have been baptized into Messiah Yeshua have been baptized into His death? Therefore we have been buried with Him through baptism into death, so that as Messiah was raised from the dead through the glory of the Father, so we too might walk in newness of life. (Romans 6:3–4)

There are also aspects of this new identity that are more mystical than legal. As believers, we are given a portion of God's Holy Spirit to dwell within us. We actually become temples of the Holy Spirit. The Holy Spirit that dwells within us is the same Spirit that dwelled within and anointed Yeshua. Therefore, we say it is the Spirit of Yeshua that dwells within us. Indeed, "Messiah in you [is] the hope of glory." (Colossians 1:27) Messiah is being formed within you. Messiah dwells "in your hearts through faith." (Ephesians 3:17) "Do you not recognize this about yourselves, that Yeshua Messiah is in you?" (2 Corinthians 13:5)

Our new creation identity is premised on the notion that the Messiah now dwells within us, is being formed within us, and lives through us. This raises a very important implication. There is a Torah-observant, Jewish guy dwelling within you!

To the extent that we surrender our lives to this new inner identity, we succeed in living out our lives in Messiah. When we show the love of Yeshua to others, it is not our love we are manifesting, but the Master's love made manifest through us. Because Messiah dwells within us, our acts of love are actually His acts of love. We become, as it were, the hands and feet of Messiah. Our new nature—our Messianic nature—is revealed.

The same is true for every act of righteousness that we perform. Our good works are credited to Messiah. It is not us, but Messiah, who lives through us.

When we continue in our old ways, walking in sin and lawlessness, we are living in contradiction to our new nature. Messiah within us is concealed. Our new identity is obscured.

When we keep the Torah, we allow Messiah to live through us. He is righteousness, and Torah is the standard of righteousness. He is the law fulfilled, and He desires to fulfill it through us.

THE TORAH MADE FLESH

In the first chapter of his gospel, the Apostle John tells us that Messiah is the incarnate Word of God—He is the "Word made flesh." (vs. 14) Through this Divine Word, all things have been made. There are all sorts of deep, philosophical, theological and mystical implications in these statements. But on its simplest level, it seems that the Apostle John was speaking of Torah. To him, the Word of God is first and foremost the Torah. He invokes the whole of the Torah with the words "In the beginning was the Word…" (vs. 1) and he returns to Torah in verse 17 with his parallel statement: "For the Law [Torah] was given through Moses; grace and truth were realized through Yeshua Messiah."

The Torah stands as the quintessential Word of God. The Torah is the Word that God spoke. All things are made through God's Word because He spoke His Word (as recorded in Torah), and all things came into being. The Torah is the will and wisdom of God, His self-disclosure to the world. As such, it is the extension of His being. In Jewish literature from around the first century, Torah is described as the Wisdom and the Word of God.

> I am the Word which was spoken by the Most High; it was I who covered the earth like a mist…All this is the covenant book of God Most High, the Torah which Moses enacted. (Sirach 24)

It is a short distance to go from a formulation like the one above where God is seen to be working in concert with the Torah, creating the world through the auspices of the Torah, to the expression we find in John 1:2. We need only remember that the Torah of God is His Word. Rabbinic literature makes that identification explicit on a number of occasions. It is most likely this exalted view of the Torah that John had in mind as he formulated his prologue.

This is not to suggest that the Divine Word that was with God from the beginning is the actual written Torah as Moses knew it or even as we know it. Rather, the distinct essence of God—projected into the void and by which creation was created, ordered and intersected—is the same essence that revealed the words of Torah to Moses and inhabited the body of Messiah. The self-revelation of God that resulted in the Torah of Moses at Sinai is the same self-revelation of God that created the universe. He is the light that shines in the darkness. He is the Torah made flesh.

This reading is consistent with how the earliest believers understood Messiah. Clement of Alexandria, one of the early Church Fathers, quotes a passage he ascribes to Peter when he says, "And in the preaching of Peter you may find the Lord is called 'Torah and Word.'"[70]

Yeshua is not the same as the written Torah of Moses. But He is of the same essence as the Torah. It is more accurate to speak of the five books of the Torah of Moses as the "Written Torah" and Yeshua as the "Living Torah." He is the Living Torah in that He emanates from the same source as the written Torah; that is, God's divine Word. He is the Living Torah in that His sinless life is lived in perfect accordance with the Torah. His life answers all that is in the written Torah.

When we become believers, this Living Torah takes up residence inside us. He is the definition of our new identity. It stands to reason then that He leads us to keep the written Torah. The written Torah and the Living Torah are meant to work hand in hand. They work in concert to reveal the Word of God through us. "For the Law [Torah] was given through Moses; grace and truth were realized through Yeshua Messiah." (John 1:17)

The promise of the new covenant is this: "I will put My law [Torah] within them and on their heart I will write it; and I will be their God, and they shall be My people." (Jeremiah 31:33) The Living Torah is writing the written Torah onto our hearts. That is Messiah being formed in us.

FAIREST OF THEM ALL

The Torah is like a mirror that shows us the face of Messiah within us. When we look into the Torah, we see the Master. He is on every page of it. He is the fulfillment of it. Each commandment is an indication of how He lived His life and desires to live through us. Our highest goal in life should be to allow the inner Christ to work through our outer man. Yet this is not possible so long as we suppose that the inner Christ would have us live in violation of the Torah that He keeps.

We do not keep the Torah in order to merit salvation. The Torah is inadequate for that. We should keep Torah because we are saved.

When we obey the instructions we find in the Bible, then (James tells us) we will be blessed in all that we do. When we look into the mirror and ask, "Mirror, mirror on the wall, who's the fairest of them all?" the soul mirror will tell us, "The One within you, living through you, is the fairest of them all."

8

The Sabbath of Torah

There is a law in the Torah that says, "Anything lost by your countryman, which he has lost and you have found...you are not allowed to neglect...You shall restore it to him." (Deuteronomy 22:2-3) I have found something that you have lost, and I hope to restore it to you. The thing I have found is the Torah. It is the same Torah that the disciples of Yeshua possessed.

The writings of the New Testament are clear about this. The followers of Yeshua were Torah people. Yeshua Himself was a Torah teacher. He told His disciples to keep and teach the Torah, and He encouraged them to demonstrate their love for Him by being faithful to the commandments.[71] His disciples were once described as many myriads, "all zealous for the Law [Torah]."[72] But through the long years of waiting for His return, we have wandered far, forgotten much and lost some things that once were of great value to us. In some ways, we have lost the Torah and forgotten that it ever belonged to us.

Torah for Christians

Torah is for Christians. The proof is that Christians keep Torah. You may not be entirely aware of it, but it is true. Just by living the Christian life, you are keeping most of the Torah. It is pretty obvious when you think it over. Consider the Ten Commandments, for example. Things like honoring one's father and mother, marital fidelity and basic honesty are all commandments of Torah. The commands to love your neighbor as yourself, care for the orphan and widow, look after the poor and extend a helping hand to a brother in need—those are all precepts of Torah. Prohibitions on violence, injustice, theft, homicide, sexual deviancy and occult practices are all examples of the basic moral statutes that comprise the laws of Torah. Faith, grace, repentance, confession, prayer and baptism are all found in the Torah too. The things that define Christian life are Torah-based. For the most part, the Christian life is one of Torah lived out.

True, there are a lot of commandments in the Torah that are not part of the normal Christian life. For example, there are the numerous animal sacrifices of the Temple worship system. Christians don't bring sacrifices. But wait! Did you know that the Torah forbids us to bring sacrifices? According to the books of Leviticus and Deuteronomy, sacrifices can only be made at the Temple in Jerusalem.[73] There has not been a Temple in Jerusalem since the days of the Apostles. It would be a sin to offer animal sacrifices today. The Bible says so. Therefore, every time we do not offer up burnt offerings in our backyard, we are keeping a commandment of the Torah: the commandment not to offer a sacrifice outside of the Temple in Jerusalem. Similarly, the strict measures of Torah justice—stoning and the like—are not applicable unless one is in the land of Israel under the authority of a duly ordained Torah court of law like the Sanhedrin. Since there has not been a functional Sanhedrin wielding civil authority in almost 2,000 years, there has not been a capital case tried in just as long. As much as we might sometimes like to stone someone, the Torah forbids us from vigilante justice of that sort. Most of the laws of Torah that Christians do not keep are laws that do not apply to us in the modern world. This is not to say that those laws are irrelevant or done away with, but under current circumstances, they cannot be practiced.

Meanwhile, Christians are busily keeping the weighty matters of the Torah all over the world. Christianity has spread the faith in the God of Abraham, Isaac and Jacob to all nations. Christians everywhere are working to see justice done, to see the oppressed relieved, to see the hungry fed and to see the Kingdom of God advanced. Christians are famous for offering care and assistance to the stranger, orphan and widow. The world may not want to admit it, but Christians are known for their high level of integrity, their moral character and their scrupulous honesty. The church has some dark chapters in its history, and there are always a few bad eggs in the basket, but overall, Christians are respected, even if they are not appreciated. All of those things are the result of Christians doing the Torah.

It seems that Christians are Torah-observant without even knowing it—well, almost. There are a few discrepancies that have arisen over the years—a few elements of Torah that we have forgotten. They are things that we lost in the early years of persecution.

Some Things Were Lost

We lost a few things early in the development of the religion. The young, emerging Christian church was deeply impacted by the First and Second Jewish Revolts against Rome.[74] In response to the Jewish uprisings, the Roman government under the Flavian emperors and again under Trajan and Hadrian unleashed punishing persecutions against Judaism. Heavy taxes combined with anti-Torah legislation, arrests and persecutions made it very unpopular to be identified with Torah or Judaism. At certain times, a person could be arrested for keeping the Sabbath or any other obvious Jewish practices. At the same time, there was a concentrated effort within Judaism to push the Messianic believers out of the synagogue. The result was that Christianity lost much of her connection to Torah and the Jewish people. This happened in fulfillment of the Master's words.

Yeshua predicted the persecutions, and He predicted the coming time of lawlessness. He told His disciples:

> They will deliver you to tribulation, and will kill you, and you will be hated by all nations because of My name. At that time many will fall away and will betray one another and hate one another. Many false prophets will arise and will mislead many. Because lawlessness [Torahlessness] is increased, most people's love will grow cold. (Matthew 24:9–12)

The love which He spoke of was the love of God—the greatest commandment. According to Deuteronomy 6:4–5, love for God is demonstrated by obedience to His commandments. Similarly, 1 John 5:3 states that "...the love of God [is] that we keep His commandments." When we began to turn away from the commandments, our love for God diminished, and as our love for God diminished, we turned from the commandments.

However, many Christians held on to Torah. The writings of the Church Fathers and the writings of the rabbis attest to the existence of Torah-keeping believers well into the third century and beyond. But most of us were assimilated into the mainstream of acceptability in the Roman world. This meant leaving behind some of the old ways.

In this chapter and the one following, we will look at a few of the things we have lost along the way. We will consider the biblical Sabbath, the biblical festivals and the biblical dietary laws.

The Biblical Sabbath

Every Friday night I watch my six-year-old daughter light the Sabbath candles to welcome the Lord's day of rest. The house is full of good smells; hot soup, a pie in the oven, fresh bread. As dusk settles on the neighborhood the boys are reading through the weekly Torah portion, preparing to contribute something at the Sabbath table. Guests arrive at the door. My wife finishes the final preparations in the kitchen. She will not need to cook again for more than twenty-four hours. At the table, prayers are said, blessings are dispensed, songs are sung and words of Torah are exchanged. The day of rest, the Lord's day, has begun.

God commands His people to cease from labor on the seventh day of the week. This day of rest is called the *Shabbat* or the Sabbath. In the Gospels, Yeshua told us, "The Son of Man is Lord of the Sabbath." (Luke 6:5) Paul says that the Sabbath is a shadow of things to come and the substance of it is Messiah.[75] Both of them are saying the same thing; that the Sabbath is about the Messiah. Therefore, the Sabbath is for the followers of Messiah.

Blessing and Holiness

Out of all those things in this vast and unreachable reality that we know as the creation, the Sabbath was the very first thing that God set apart as holy. The Sabbath stands from the beginning of time as the first institution of godliness. Before there was a temple or an altar, before there was a Bible or a commandment, before there was a church or a single hymn was written, there was the Sabbath.

For believers who keep the Sabbath, it is our delight, the day of our joy. It is our treasure and prized possession. It is the oldest heirloom we have inherited from the family of God.

As followers of the Master, when we begin to enter into His Sabbath, we encounter Him in fresh, new and delightful ways. The Sabbath is not burdensome as some suppose. The Lord of the Sabbath declares, "Come to Me, all who are weary and heavy-laden, and I will give you rest." (Matthew 11:28)

For us, the Sabbath is a gift, not a despotic ruler demanding our submission. It is gentle and beckoning, subtle and sublime, wrapped in garments of light, inviting us to meet with the Lord. We delight in the Sabbath because we encounter Yeshua within it.

The Sabbath of Peace

The Sabbath is a day of peace. It is a time for setting aside the troubles of our world. On the Sabbath, we close the door to the troubles, stresses and anxieties of this present age and we enter into the calm spirit of peace that comes from the presence of Messiah. "Peace I leave with you; My peace I give to you; not as the world gives do I give to you. Do not let your heart be troubled, nor let it be fearful," (John 14:27) says the Master. On the Sabbath day, we quiet ourselves enough to feel the presence of His peace.

In Colossians 2, Paul claims that the Sabbath is a shadow of things to come.[76] The book of Revelation tells us that the coming of Messiah will institute a 1,000-year era of peace—the Kingdom on earth. This 1,000-year era can be compared to the Sabbath. Bible teachers often point out how the six days of the week can be likened to the 6,000 years of redemptive history. "With the Lord one day is like a thousand years, and a thousand years like one day," (2 Peter 3:8) Peter reminds us. The seventh-day Sabbath is therefore likened to the millennial reign of Messiah.

These are not just Christian ideas. Even the rabbis of old believed that the Sabbath was a foreshadowing of the age of peace that Messiah will bring.[77]

The prophets tell us that when Messiah comes, all mankind will keep the Sabbath. "'From sabbath to sabbath, all mankind will come to bow down before Me,' says the Lord." (Isaiah 66:23) Every time we keep the Sabbath, it is a little foretaste of the perfect Sabbath rest that will be ours when Messiah comes.

THE SABBATH OF CREATION

When God rested on the seventh day, He ceased from His work. The Hebrew word for cessation is *shabbat*. The word Sabbath comes from *shabbat*. When God rested, He did not cease from work because He was exhausted after six days of creating. He ceased from work because the work was done. The original context of creation makes it clear that the work God rested from on the Sabbath is the work of creation. Therefore, on the Sabbath day, we rest from the work of creating as well. We cease from the work of shaping, creating, forming, making, ordering, structuring, organizing, mixing, and molding things to produce results. Imposing our will onto substance, and creating order from disorder, is work. Production is work. Creation is work. Making money is work. We cease from work as a remembrance of creation, and we cease from work to remember our salvation.

THE SABBATH OF SALVATION

To Yeshua, the Sabbath was His Father's day. There could be no better day for seeing salvation accomplished in the lives of men and women. That is why He ignored the conventional religious wisdom and insisted on healing on the Sabbath day. The Sabbath is the Lord's day; what better day to receive a touch from God? What better day to meet the man named Salvation (Yeshua)?

As believers, we rest in Messiah. Hebrews chapters 3 and 4 teach us that the Sabbath is a picture of the eternal life we posses through faith in Yeshua. It compares our salvation to the Sabbath. Those without faith in Yeshua, the writer of Hebrews explains, are like those without rest. He says, "There remains a Sabbath rest for the people of God. For the one who has entered His rest [the Sabbath] has himself also rested from his works, as God did from His." (Hebrews 4:9–10) God rested on the seventh day because the work of creation was finished. So too we can rest in our salvation because the work of Messiah is finished. The Sabbath, according to the writer of Hebrews, is a picture of grace.

When we keep the Lord's Sabbath, we rest from our work. In the same way, when we place faith in Messiah, we rest from striving to earn salvation. We can be confident that the work is finished. We can rest in the certainty of His grace.

THE SABBATH OF GRACE

The Sabbath is a beautiful picture of grace. Like grace, it is a gift.

For six days we strive. For six days we try hard. For six days life is about our works and deeds. Six days you shall labor and do all your work to support yourself and your family. For six days we strive to impose our wills onto creation, shaping, creating, forming, making, ordering, structuring, organizing, mixing and molding—producing results. But on the seventh day, we stop. By stopping for a day, we acknowledge God. By keeping the Sabbath, I acknowledge that it is not by my own hand nor by my own power but by His hand and power that I am sustained and provided for. Sabbath is the day when I acknowledge that I am not the creator, the maker, or the shaper. I am not God. He is the one who provides for me, not my efforts.

This is the message of God's grace as well. Though we strive to be good enough, to clear the bar of righteousness, the reality is that we are merely human. On our own, we can never be righteous enough to make the grade. Our works of righteousness will never be adequate to merit our own redemption.

When salvation comes, we realize the work is over. It is done. God says, "Rest. Enter My rest because the work is done. Not because you finished it; because I finished it. It is already accomplished. Now just rest."

We rest in the perfection of His new creation. We rest in the finished work of His Son. Yeshua said it from the cross: "It is finished." (John 19:30) It is done. There is nothing we can add to it. Just rest in it. There is nothing we can do to improve on it. Just rest in it. That is grace, and that is what the Sabbath is like.

SABBATH OF FREEDOM

Sometimes it is hard to rest in grace. We want to shape just one more thing. We want to control just one more thing. We say, "Please God, let me impose my will on just one more thing." There is a sale at the mall. There is a roast still in the freezer. There is overtime available at work.

Sometimes it is hard to stop and rest because our busy schedules drive us like Pharaoh. "More bricks, more bricks, and get your own darn straw!" Pharaoh says. How can we take a break when we have all these bricks to make? We don't have time.

The commandment of Sabbath forces us to stop for one day and remember. Who created time? Who set time in motion? Who set the spheres revolving? Sabbath is the one day out of a week to remember that we serve God, not Pharaoh. We are God's servants. We keep the Sabbath because He has set us free, and as freed men and women, we are able to keep His holy day.

Sabbath of Messiah

It stands to reason that if Yeshua is the Lord of the Sabbath, and if the substance of the Sabbath is Messiah, then the Sabbath is for the followers of Yeshua. Every Sabbath is traditionally initiated with the cup and bread, just like Passover. Deuteronomy instructs us to keep the Sabbath as a remembrance of the exodus from Egypt.[78] In its own small way, every Sabbath is like a little Passover feast. It was at Passover that Yeshua told us to take the cup and bread in remembrance of Him. Therefore, every time we keep the Sabbath day, it is a remembrance of Messiah.

He is our blessing and holiness, our deep peace and our sure salvation. He is our new creation, our source of grace and our great freedom. He is our Sabbath rest; thus we rest on the Sabbath in Him.

The Sabbath-Breaker

"But wait! Jesus was a Sabbath-breaker, wasn't He?"

Well, that's what His enemies among the Pharisees claimed. They said, "This man is not from God, because He does not keep the Sabbath." (John 9:16) His enemies wanted to prove that He was a Sabbath-breaker because, according to the Torah, breaking the Sabbath is a sin. If they could prove that He was a sinner, they could prove that He was not the Messiah.

The same allegation is still being lodged against Yeshua nearly 2,000 years later. "Jesus broke the Sabbath!" But this time it is His followers, not His enemies, who accuse Him of Sabbath-breaking. Why are Christians so eager to affirm with the Pharisees' allegations?

From a simple reading of the Gospels, it does seem that Yeshua must have been a Sabbath-breaker. His disciples plucked grain on the Sabbath; He defended them. He healed people on the Sabbath. He told a man to carry his mat home on the Sabbath. He made mud and applied it as salve to a blind man's eyes on the Sabbath. All of these are obvious violations of the Sabbath, right? Wrong. According to the Bible, none of them are violations of the Sabbath. In fact, even in traditional Jewish law, some of these were debatable questions. Two centuries later, the rabbis of the *Talmud* were still arguing about the conditions under which it might be permissible to heal on the Sabbath, carry a load on the Sabbath, make medicine on the Sabbath or apply salve on the Sabbath.[79]

SABBATH AND SUNDAY

"But didn't Jesus move the Sabbath to Sunday?"

No. Nowhere in the Bible does it say, or even imply, that Yeshua or His followers met and worshipped on Sunday.

Keeping the Sabbath day is one of the most often-repeated commandments in the Bible. If Messiah or the Apostles meant to change the Sabbath, they would have made the change explicit, and they would have provided compelling teaching to explain why this frequently repeated commandment of the law no longer applies. They did not. In fact, neither Yeshua nor the Apostles regarded Sunday as the Sabbath day. It is not in the Bible. The move to Sunday happened after the days of the Apostles.

Sometimes teachers point to Acts 20:7 which says, "On the first of the week, when we were gathered together to break bread...." But this passage is a reference to a Sabbath-end (Saturday) meal, such as is still practiced in Judaism today. Remember that the biblical day begins in the evening. In Jewish reckoning, the first of the week begins on Saturday night, not Sunday morning. This is quite explicit in the Greek of Acts 20.

It is customary for Torah communities to gather on Saturday night, at the end of the Sabbath and beginning of the new week. Even in Orthodox Jewish communities today, it is customary for disciples of a particular rabbi to gather around their teacher on Saturday night to bid farewell to the Sabbath and to welcome the new week with words of Torah. The Troas community in Acts 20 was doing the same. The rest of the story bears this out. That's why Paul spoke all night, not all day, and that's why Eutychus fell asleep and out of the window.

Sometimes teachers point to the obscure mention of John walking on the Isle of Patmos on the Lord's Day.[80] "Doesn't that prove that Sunday was regarded as the Lord's Day?" No. No mention of Sunday is made in the passage.

It is not wrong to worship and assemble on Sunday, but Sunday is not the Sabbath, and we should not suppose that it was Yeshua's idea.

Yeshua's Attitude toward the Sabbath

If Yeshua did not change the Sabbath, and if Yeshua was not a Sabbath-breaker (and He certainly was not), then what was His attitude about the Sabbath? When we read the Bible from a Hebraic perspective, it becomes clear that the Sabbath mattered a great deal to Yeshua. Think of how many stories from the Gospels are set on the Sabbath day. Yeshua performed many of His most important miracles on Sabbaths. The Gospels tell us that it was Yeshua's custom to go to the synagogue every Sabbath.[81] That is because the Sabbath is supposed to be the day of assembly.[82] The Greek word *synagogue* means "assembly." We see Him celebrating Sabbath with meals among the Pharisees,[83] and we see Him spending Sabbath among the disciples. To Yeshua, the Sabbath was the day of rest, the day of redemption and healing and the day of His Father. The only work He did on the Sabbath was the work of redemption, the work of God His Father.[84] It was a day for healing human bodies and souls.

He often knocked heads with religious authorities over how one should keep the Sabbath. The religious authorities of His day were locked into heated arguments of their own over how to keep the Sabbath properly. Yeshua was concerned with restoring a balanced perspective regarding Sabbath observance. His conflict with the Pharisees over the particulars of how one ought to observe the Sabbath shows that the Sabbath was an important institution to

Him. Far from dismissing the Sabbath or telling His disciples to disregard it, He was concerned that the Sabbath be kept according to the spirit in which God gave it.

As Yeshua endeavored to teach His disciples about their relationship to the Sabbath, He told them, "The Sabbath was made for man, and not man for the Sabbath." (Mark 2:27) On another occasion He contrasted His Sabbath observance with that of His opponents by saying, "Come to Me, all who are weary and heavy-laden, and I will give you rest. Take My yoke upon you and learn from Me, for I am gentle and humble in heart, and you will find rest for your souls. For My yoke is easy and my burden is light." (Matthew 11:28–30) The famous passage is followed immediately by an example of His more lenient attitude about Sabbath observance.

Yeshua told His disciples to pray that their flight from Jerusalem would not take place on a Sabbath day.[85] Even the rabbis allow for one to flee on the Sabbath in order to save one's life. But Yeshua told His disciples to pray that they would not need to break the Sabbath to save their lives. Those do not sound like the words of a Sabbath-breaker.

Yeshua told them, "The Son of Man is Lord of the Sabbath." (Luke 6:5) Would the Lord of the Sabbath not keep the Sabbath? On another occasion He told them, "The Son can do nothing of Himself, unless *it is* something He sees the Father doing; for whatever the Father does, these things the Son also does in like manner." (John 5:19) This being the standard, Yeshua certainly kept the Sabbath. After all, it was God His Father who first rested on the Sabbath and declared it blessed and holy.

According to the Commandment

If there is any doubt about what Yeshua taught His disciples regarding the Sabbath, we need only look into the story of His burial. The Bible says, in the Gospel of Luke, that the Sabbath was about to begin as the tomb was closed.

> The Sabbath was about to begin. Now the women who had come with Him out of Galilee followed, and saw the tomb and how His body was laid. Then they returned and prepared spices and perfumes. And on the Sabbath they rested according to the commandment. (Luke 23:54–56)

To the disciples of Yeshua, the Sabbath was so holy that they would not even violate it for the sake of attending to His body. Had Yeshua taught them to disregard the Sabbath, they would not have been concerned with resting "according to the commandment." No power on earth could have stood between the women and the body of their beloved Teacher. But Yeshua had taught them to revere the Sabbath, and revere it they did. Even though it meant waiting an extra day before they could pay honor to the body of the Master, "on the Sabbath they rested according to the commandment."

A Day of Rest for All God's Children

After His death and resurrection, the community of His disciples continued in His ways, and they kept the Sabbath. Some might suppose that Yeshua and his Jewish followers kept the Sabbath because they were Jewish, and that the Sabbath is not meant for non-Jewish believers. After all, there is no mention of the Sabbath in Acts 15's mandates for non-Jews. According to the Bible, though, the Sabbath is meant for all Israel; for the Jew, the stranger, the foreigner and all flesh alike.[86] The prophet Isaiah tells us that in the end times, those non-Jews who keep the Sabbath day will be given a place in God's holy Temple.

> Also the foreigners who join themselves to the Lord, to minister to Him, and to love the name of the Lord, to be His servants, every one who keeps from profaning the sabbath and holds fast My covenant; even those I will bring to My holy mountain and make them joyful in My house of prayer. (Isaiah 56:6–7)

Paul's non-Jewish converts met in the synagogues. In Acts 15, James mentions that Gentiles will hear Torah in the synagogues on the Sabbath day.[87] This implies that they were already keeping the Sabbath before the mandates of Acts 15. It also implies that the Apostles assumed that they would continue to do so. There was no other day of worship.

The numerous stories told in the Gospels about Yeshua's healing work on the Sabbath and His arguments over the Sabbath demonstrate that Sabbath-related issues were still very relevant to the believers for whom the Gospels were written. They were keeping the Sabbath, and they wanted to know what Yeshua did on the Sabbath. It mattered to them, and that is why those stories are in the Bible.

Unfortunately, when those same stories are read outside the context of a Sabbath-keeping faith, we misinterpret them to mean that Yeshua was a Sabbath-breaker. It is a misreading that would play well into the hands of His detractors. If Yeshua was a Sabbath-breaker, then His enemies among the Pharisees were correct. He was a sinner, and He could not be the Messiah. Our faith is in vain.

But we know that He was without sin. Therefore, we know that He kept the Sabbath as the Gospels indicate. He kept the Sabbath and He taught His disciples to keep the Sabbath. After all, He is the one who said of Himself, "The Son of Man is Lord of the Sabbath."

9

The Festivals of Torah

For Christians today, our true identity has been largely forgotten. The ways of the early believers are lost. How shocking to discover that we are not the people we thought we were, but the sons and daughters of royalty. Through our adoption into the family of God, we are partakers with the Jewish people in a great legacy. In Messiah, Abraham is our father, and Sarah is our mother. We hail from the Holy City of Jerusalem. We are of the exalted line of King David, and Yeshua our brother is the King Himself. The Bible is our heritage, including the Torah and all the ways of the household of God. The things of Torah tell us about our family. They are our inheritance, our biblical heritage. We need only take hold of it and claim it for ourselves.

God's Calendar

We have already learned about the biblical Sabbath. It is a large component of our lost heritage. The Bible refers to the Sabbath as one of God's appointed times. But there are several other appointed times on the biblical calendar as well.

In Leviticus 23, God gives a calendar to His people. This biblical calendar is different from the one to which we are accustomed. The biblical calendar is lunar. That means it is based on the phases of the moon. The waxing and waning of the moon determines the day of the biblical month. The tiny sliver of the new moon is always the first day of the month, the full moon indicates the middle of the month, and the disappearance of the moon indicates the end of the month.

God declares certain days to be His appointed times. He says, "The Lord's appointed times which you shall proclaim as holy convocations—My appointed times are these." (Leviticus 23:2)

What does this mean? We can understand it if we think about our own busy schedules. Many people keep a Palm Pilot or other day planner. These contain blank calendars on which to enter various appointments. Suppose you intend to meet your friend Joe at a coffee shop. You and Joe might set a time—say, Tuesday, August 17, at 2:00 p.m. You would flip open your day planner or turn on your Palm Pilot to find the calendar page that shows your schedule for Tuesday, August 17. After you determine that the 2:00 slot is open, you write in, "Coffee shop with Joe."

Leviticus 23 is like God's day planner. He has made appointments on which to meet with His people. They include the weekly Sabbath, the Feasts of Passover and Pentecost, the Feast of Trumpets, the Day of Atonement and the Feast of Booths. They are His appointments. Unlike our day planners and easily deleted Palm Pilot entries, God's day planner does not change.

When we are uncertain about whether or not we will be able to keep an appointment, we might say, "I'll pencil it in." The implication is that if things change and we are unable to keep the appointment, we can change our plans. With God, there is no uncertainty about His schedule. You might say He doesn't even own a pencil. When He wrote out His day planner, He wrote in ink, and the ink has been dry for 3,400 years. His Palm Pilot is etched into His palm.

But in what sense are these festivals to be regarded as God's appointed times? What are they for? They are the times for God to do business with us. Let's take a brief look at these appointed times.

Passover and the Lamb

After the weekly Sabbath, Passover is the first appointed time on the Leviticus 23 calendar. On the first Passover, God told His people to slaughter a lamb and apply its blood to the doorpost of their homes. They were to eat the lamb with bitter herbs and unleavened bread. That night, God rescued them from Egypt and told them to keep the festival of Passover as a remembrance of their salvation from bondage and slavery. But it was more than just a remembrance. It was also a rehearsal for something wonderful to come. It was one of God's appointed times.

Yeshua went with His disciples to keep the Passover in Jerusalem 1,400 years after the exodus from Egypt. He always kept the Father's appointed times. He and His disciples had been to Jerusalem to keep the Passover many times before this occasion. But this time was different. The appointed time was going to be fulfilled in a marvelous and unexpected way. As they neared Jerusalem, Yeshua said, "My time is near; I *am to* keep the Passover." (Matthew 26:18) He kept the Passover meal (called a s*eder* meal) with His disciples. He took the unleavened bread and the customary Passover cup in a ritual Christians remember as 'the Lord's Supper.' On the day of Passover, He became the Passover lamb. At the time when Israel slaughtered their Passover lambs in remembrance of their great salvation from Egypt, Yeshua was crucified and His blood was applied as a mark of salvation on all who would believe in Him.

That's an example of how the appointed times work. They are God's appointed times for doing business. They are His appointed times for the work of redemption. They teach us about the work of Yeshua. That is why Paul told the Corinthians to keep Messiah in mind as they celebrated the feast. He reminds us that, as we cast out the leaven in order to keep the Feast of Unleavened Bread, we need to cast out the sin that works like leaven in our lives.

> Clean out the old leaven so that you may be a new lump, just as you are *in fact* unleavened. For Messiah our Passover also has been sacrificed. Therefore let us celebrate the feast, not with old leaven, nor with the leaven of malice and wickedness, but with the unleavened bread of sincerity and truth. (1 Corinthians 5:7–8)

Every year, as my family keeps the festival of Passover (the Feast of Unleavened Bread), we do so in remembrance of Yeshua. After all, Messiah Himself told us to keep the Passover in remembrance of Him (Luke 22:19). Was it just breaking bread and drinking the fruit of the vine that He had in mind? No. There was a specific context, and the context was Passover. In Luke He said, "I have earnestly desired to eat this Passover with you before I suffer; for I say to you, I shall never again eat it until it is fulfilled in the kingdom of God." (Luke 22:15–16)

The commandment to do "this" in remembrance of Yeshua is not a commandment just to take a cup and some bread. The specific "this" to which Yeshua referred was the Passover *seder* meal. It is not one cup, but the traditional cups of Passover. It is not any bread; it is the unleavened *matzah* bread of Passover. What could be more appropriate for a disciple of Yeshua to do than to keep the festival of Passover in remembrance of Him, just as He told His disciples?

As believers keeping the Passover, we can use the annual remembrance of our Savior's suffering as a time to renew our lives in Him. We will do well to take the Apostle Paul's advice and "cast out the old leaven," both from our homes and from our lives.

The Barley Sheaf and the Resurrection

The next appointed time on God's Leviticus 23 calendar is a special day that falls during the week of Passover (Unleavened Bread). The Torah tells Israel to bring a sheaf of the first ripened grain to the Temple as a first fruits offering to the Lord. It is to be brought on "the day after the sabbath." [88]

The command to bring the first sheaf (*omer*) of the harvest to the Temple should be of great significance to Christians. This obscure appointment on the biblical calendar—sometimes called the First Fruits of the Barley Harvest—is a minor festival with major Messianic implications.

On the same day that Yeshua was tried before the priests and judges of the Sanhedrin, apostles of the Sanhedrin were sent out to a barley field not far from Jerusalem. On the same day that Yeshua was bound and crucified, the apostles of the Sanhedrin bound up the standing barley into bundles while it was still attached to the ground so that it would be easier to reap. [89] The day leading up to Yeshua's resurrection, they reaped the barley, collected it and brought it to Jerusalem. The harvest ritual of gathering this barley sheaf was for a special first fruits offering to the Lord. According to Torah, no one could use or eat grain and produce from the new year's crops until a sheaf of the first grain to ripen was harvested and brought to the Temple. Barley is the first crop to ripen in Israel, so the offering was always a barley sheaf. The commandment of the barley sheaf served to remind Israel that the land and its produce belonged first to God. The produce of the land could not be enjoyed until God had received His due acknowledgement.

By divine design, the rituals of offering the first fruits sheaf in the Temple coincided with the death and resurrection of Yeshua. Perhaps this is what the Apostle Paul had in mind when he declared, "But now Messiah has been raised from the dead, the first fruits of those who are asleep." (1 Corinthians 15:20) Obviously, the celebration of the first fruits of the barley—the resurrection of Messiah—is important for the disciples of Yeshua.

PENTECOST AND THE FIRE ON THE MOUNTAIN

The next appointment on God's Leviticus 23 calendar occurs fifty days after the first fruits sheaf of grain was offered at the Temple. It is called the Feast of Pentecost (*Shavuot*). Pentecost means "fifty."

Before it was a New Testament event, the Jewish Sages considered Pentecost to be the anniversary of the day God spoke the Torah at Mount Sinai. In Judaism, it is called the festival of the "Giving of the Torah." Before tongues of fire ever fell upon the believers in Jerusalem, there was fire falling on Mount Sinai. As the disciples of the risen Messiah were gathering to celebrate Pentecost in Jerusalem, they were gathering to celebrate the anniversary of the giving of the Torah.

Let's consider the significance of the first Pentecost at Mount Sinai. Exodus 19 and 20 tells the story. God stepped down from the heavens; He stepped onto the top of a mountain. There was wind; there was lighting; there was thunder; there was smoke; there was the very loud sound of a ram's horn trumpet blowing, and there was fire. The entire nation audibly heard the voice of God speaking the Ten Commandments.

According to Jewish legend, when God spoke the Ten Commandments on Mount Sinai, His voice spoke forth in all the languages of mankind and it took the shape of fiery sparks that encircled the camp of Israel and came to rest on each individual Jew. [90]

Is that how it really happened? It does not matter whether the legends are true. Perhaps God's voice did speak in every language. Perhaps it did not. Perhaps His words came forth as fiery sparks that rested on each individual. Perhaps they did not. It is important, however, to remember that Peter and the disciples and followers of Yeshua were all well aware of the Pentecost legends. They must have known the story of the giving of the Torah on Pentecost. They knew the story of the words of fire resting on each individual. They knew the story of God's voice speaking to all mankind in every language. Therefore, the miracles, signs and wonders that came upon them in Acts chapter two carried deep significance. The tongues of fire and the speaking in every tongue were both direct allusions to the Mount Sinai experience and the receiving of the Torah.

It is as if God drew a line of connection between the giving of His Torah and the giving of His Spirit. We are not to see the one without considering the other. The two events are interconnected. God's Spirit and His Law are related.

As you can see, Pentecost is relevant to the disciples of Messiah. That is why they gathered together for Pentecost. That is why Paul hurried across the Mediterranean to arrive in Jerusalem for the festival of Pentecost.[91]

THE FEAST OF TRUMPETS

There are other important appointments on God's Leviticus 23 calendar. They are the fall holidays of the Feast of Trumpets, the Day of Atonement and the Feast of Booths. The Feast of Trumpets is a day on which the Torah tells us to celebrate by blowing a ram's horn trumpet. It is a festival that is meant to prepare us for the holy Day of Atonement that comes ten days later. In Jewish tradition, the Feast of Trumpets is regarded as the New Year (*Rosh HaShanah*). It is a day for reconciliation between friends and families. It is a day when Torah-keeping people review the previous year's sins and shortcomings, and make a special effort to apologize to one another and forgive one another. It is a day for hearing the ram's horn trumpet (*shofar*) blown.

For disciples of the Messiah, the Feast of Trumpets is a reminder of that appointed time yet to come when the Master "will send forth His angels with a great trumpet and they will gather together His elect from the four winds, from one end of the sky to the other." (Matthew 24:31) It is a day on which we anticipate the coming judgment, the trumpets of the book of Revelation, and the beginning of the end. It is a glimpse of the future to come, a shadow cast through time. As such, it is relevant for everyone who believes in Messiah's return. It is an important festival for the disciples of Yeshua.

THE DAY OF ATONEMENT

The next appointed time on God's Leviticus 23 calendar occurs ten days after the Feast of Trumpets. It is the Day of Atonement (*Yom Kippur*). The Bible says, "It is on this day that atonement shall be made for you to cleanse you; you will be clean from all your sins before the Lord." (Leviticus 16:30) The Day of Atonement is the holiest day of the year. Its exalted holiness arises from the fact that it is the anniversary of the day on which the holiest man in the world used to enter the holiest place in the world. The holiest man in the world was the high priest of Israel. The holiest place was the Holy of Holies in the Temple. Every year, on the Day of Atonement, the high priest used to enter the Holy of Holies and apply the atoning blood of the sin offerings.

The book of Hebrews says that this day teaches us about the work of Messiah on our behalf. He is our High Priest—not in the Temple on earth, but in the heavenly Temple. He carried His own blood into the Holy of Holies of the heavenly Temple.

Jewish custom refers to the Day of Atonement as Judgment Day because of its biblical associations with sin, atonement and forgiveness. The traditional synagogue Day of Atonement service lasts most of the day. Since it is a fast day, the whole day is spent in prayer, confession, study and reflection. Most Torah-keeping communities of believers spend the day together and break the fast together at the end of the day. For disciples of Yeshua, the Day of Atonement is a special and significant day. It is the day we rehearse Yeshua's work on our behalf. On this, the holiest day of the year, we concern ourselves with the cleansing, atoning work of Messiah that has wrought for us forgiveness, pardon and right standing with God. Prayers of confession are a key component. The Gospels and the Epistles frequently enjoin us to confess our sins. The Day of Atonement is a day set aside for deliberate, intentional and conscientious confession of sin. It is a 24-hour period of devotional introspection during which we scrutinize our behavior, confess our shortcomings, and throw ourselves on the mercy and grace of our great King. Spending a Day of Atonement among believers who take the day seriously is an amazing, life-changing experience. It is relevant for every disciple of Messiah.

The Festival of Booths (Feast of Tabernacles)

The last appointment on God's Leviticus 23 calendar is the Feast of Booths, an eight-day harvest celebration. The Hebrew name of the festival is *Sukkot*, a word that means "shelters, stables or huts." These temporary, tent-like structures are often translated as "tabernacles" in our English Bibles. The festival is so named because Israel is commanded to annually build such dwelling places as a reminder of the post-exodus years when they lived in huts and booths, following God in the wilderness.[92] Many beautiful traditions are attached to the annual Festival of Booths. For example, it is traditional to invite guests into one's booth for a festive meal each night of the festival. Among the list of invitees are some auspicious names: Abraham, Isaac, Jacob, Joseph, Moses, Aaron and David. Each are specially invited to come into the booth and pull up a chair at the table. Obviously, Abraham, Isaac, Jacob, Joseph, Moses, Aaron and David are unlikely to actually attend the meal, since they are all dead. That, however, is the point of the ritual. The Feast of Booths anticipates the Messianic Age when the dead will be raised to life again and we will all sit at the table with the aforementioned in the Kingdom of Heaven. In that day, each man will take shelter under his own vine and fig tree.[93] A tabernacle of glory will be spread over Jerusalem.[94] According to the prophets, the Feast of Booths celebrates a time when all nations will ascend to Jerusalem bearing tribute to King Messiah and celebrating the festival.

> Then it will come about that any who are left of all the nations that went against Jerusalem will go up from year to year to worship the King, the LORD of hosts, and to celebrate the Feast of Booths. (Zechariah 14:16)

Many Messianic Torah teachers make a case for placing the birth of Yeshua during the Feast of Booths. Theologically, this is very compelling because, among other reasons, the Apostle John uses a verb form of the same Greek word that is used to translate booth (*sukkah*) when he wrote, "And the Word became flesh, and dwelt [tabernacled] among us." (John 1:14) He tabernacled among us then, and He will tabernacle among us again in the Messianic age. The celebration of the Festival of Booths celebrates the Messiah who once tabernacled among us, now tabernacles within us, and in the future will again tabernacle among us. In that day, all nations will ascend to His throne in Jerusalem in order to celebrate the Festival of Booths (Tabernacles). Obviously, this is a very important festival for disciples of Messiah today.

SHADOWS OF MESSIAH

When we look over the appointed times on God's calendar, it is easy to see Messiah in each appointment. This is what Paul meant when he said that the festivals are shadows of things to come and the substance of Messiah.

In Colossians 2:16–17, Paul told the Gentile believers of the city of Colossae:

> Let no one, then, judge you in eating or in drinking, or in respect of a feast, or of a new moon, or of sabbaths, which are a shadow of the coming things, and the body [is] of the Messiah. (Colossians 2:16–17, Young's Literal Translation)

Some versions of the Bible display their translators' biases. For example, the NASB inserts the word "mere" into the verse in order to diminish the importance of the biblical festivals. It then reads, "things which are a mere shadow of what is to come; but the substance belongs to Christ," implying that the festivals and laws of Torah are insubstantial and inconsequential. The New International Version translators were brazen enough to actually change the tense of the verb to the past tense so that it reads, "These are a shadow of the things that were to come; the reality, however, is found in Christ."

APPOINTED TIME	CHRISTOLOGICAL MEANING
Sabbath (*Shabbat*) Leviticus 23:2–3	Sabbath rest of creation, the final redemption and 1000-year reign of Messiah.
Passover and Unleavened Bread (*Pesach, Chag HaMatzah*) Leviticus 23:4–8	The Last Supper, Messiah our Passover Lamb, His death and burial.
First Fruits of the Barley (*Omer*) Leviticus 23:9–14	Messiah's resurrection.
Pentecost (*Shavuot*) Leviticus 23:15–21	The outpouring of Messiah's Spirit just as the Torah was given at Sinai.
Long dry summer months without appointments.	Messiah's absence.
Feast of Trumpets (*Yom Teruah, Rosh HaShanah*) Leviticus 23:23–25	The trumpet blast of the return of Messiah. The trumpets of the last days.
Day of Atonement (*Yom Kippur*) Leviticus 23:26–32	The atoning work of Messiah's blood. The day of final judgment.
The Feast of Booths (*Sukkot*) Leviticus 23:33–44	Sabbath rest of creation, the final redemption and 1,000-year reign of Messiah who will tabernacle among us.

The literal reading of the verse does not set Messiah and the things of Torah in antithesis, nor does it dismiss the matters of Torah as irrelevant relics of the past. Paul is attempting to tell the Colossian believers that the true relevance of the biblical calendar (new moons) and the biblical Sabbaths and festivals, and even the biblical dietary laws is that they are shadows of coming things and the substance (literally "body") of Messiah.

The metaphor is clear enough. Every shadow results from a shadow-caster. Messiah is the body; the biblical calendar is the shadow He casts. Paul told the Colossians not to allow people to judge them in regard to things that are substantially about Messiah. Paul was encouraging the Colossians not to allow others to judge them for keeping the biblical feasts. Those doing the judging might have been Jews or Gentiles criticizing the non-Jews for keeping Torah without first converting to Judaism.

At any rate, we should not read this passage as a dismissal of the value of keeping the festivals. Instead Paul tells us that they are a shadow of things to come and the substance of Messiah. If anything, he is encouraging us to see the true meaning of the festivals. When we realize that the substance of the appointed times is Messiah, we are more inclined to keep them. It becomes a matter of discipleship.

But God's calendar does more than testify of Messiah; it changes our lives. It is a cycle of sanctification that provides an annual pattern of growth for healthy discipleship. Every Passover we are to recount our salvation and relive the dramatic redemption that is ours in Messiah our Passover Lamb. On Pentecost we relive the vivifying reception of the Holy Spirit. At the Feast of Trumpets, we tremble in anticipation of His return and prepare our hearts for that final judgment by exercising heartfelt repentance, confession and reconciliation. On the Day of Atonement we cast ourselves on God's grace as we confess that we are unworthy of His mercy, but gratefully accept the free gift of His pardon and atonement. On the Feast of Booths we celebrate God's bounty upon us and rejoice over the work He has accomplished in our lives over the course of the year as we eagerly look forward to Messiah dwelling with us in the future.

As the disciples of the Messiah rediscover the biblical festivals, we rediscover our own heritage. We reclaim our biblical identity.

10

THE LIFE OF TORAH

Our original identity has been largely forgotten. Imagine a man on a long journey, exiled from his home and in search of a new land. On his back he has all of his belongings. It is a great load, but his back is strong and his legs are stout. Yet as he travels, he is beset by bandits. In order to escape them, he tosses some of his belongings aside. The lighter load allows him to move faster. Some time later, when he has run out of money, he finds he must barter certain items he is carrying in order to buy food for the journey. On another occasion he inadvertently leaves some precious items behind at a lodging place, not noticing the loss until much later. When his long journey is finally complete, most of the belongings he originally set out with have been lost along the way.

Such is our story. As a faith, we set out from Jerusalem 2,000 years ago on a long journey into all nations. God has been faithful and brought us to this place today. But along the way, we have lost many of the things that once were precious to us.

Among the things we left at various stages on our journey were the celebration of the Sabbath and the biblical festivals. There are several other things as well. Now, as the restoration begins, we have an opportunity to claim them.

THE MONTHLY CYCLE

Among the many things we lost on our journey from Jerusalem, we left behind the lunar calendar. Originally, believers followed a lunar calendar in determining the months, seasons and appointments because the lunar calendar is biblical. The Torah teaches that every month we are to observe and take note of the appearance of the new moon. We are to mark out the seasons and days according to its waxing and waning. As we watch the moon grow to its fullness and recede until it vanishes from the sky, it teaches us important truths about God's rhythms and cycles.

In Judaism, when the new moon appears again, it is said to be "born again." As such, it serves as a monthly reminder of spiritual rebirth.

In the ancient world, until people sighted the new moon, they were uncertain of when the month would begin. The sighting of the new moon determined the calendar, which in turn determined the days on which the festivals should occur. This teaches us an important lesson. Just as the new moon must be observed before the festivals can be celebrated, spiritual rebirth must precede any of our ritual observances.

The Torah points to an obvious connection between the monthly cycle of the moon and the monthly cycle of the human body. God has synchronized the body of the typical woman to the lunar month; so long as her menstrual cycle is regular, she will begin menstruation at the same phase of the moon each month. Human beings are the only mammals synchronized to the moon. A woman's body is uniquely tuned to God's calendar, practicing a continual cycle of rebirth and recreation.

During a woman's week of menstruation, she is technically regarded as 'unclean' by the Torah. In actual practice today, her uncleanness has no real relevance because there is no Temple. If the Temple still stood, she would not be able to participate in the worship or sacrifices that took place there until menstruation ended and she levitically cleansed herself. To become ritually clean after menstruation, a woman need only immerse herself in a ritual baptism.

Even without a Temple, menstruation is still an important matter of concern in the Torah. God expressly prohibits sexual relations for seven days after menstruation begins.[95] This is a matter of sexual morality aside from any ritual purity concerns. Abstinence for seven days following the onset of the menstrual cycle is a commandment that applies to us today.

In Orthodox Jewish communities, married women still practice a monthly ritual as a remembrance of the way things were in the Temple age. In those communities, the immersion marks the end of the period of abstinence engendered by menstruation. Husband and wife are rejoined. It is a poignant and much anticipated phase of the lunar cycle in healthy marriages, often described as a monthly honeymoon.

The woman's body, like the moon, is an ongoing picture of renewal and rebirth. Each month, a woman's body passes from life to death to life again. She passes from ritual, levitical uncleanness to levitical purity through the rite of immersion.

Messiah Himself is our baptism. In Him we are purified and renewed, allowing His life to come forth through us. In Messiah, we are born again like the moon, born again like the woman cleansed. Thus the Torah elevates the woman's monthly cycle from the level of the mundane and normal to a level of spiritual truth and transformation. Each woman becomes a monthly reminder of our spiritual renewal.

The synchronicity of the two cycles teaches us the connection between us and the lunar calendar. Not coincidently, the lunar calendar is also the biblical calendar. Our very bodies are tuned to God's biblical calendar.

Baptism

When Christians first begin to study the things of Torah, many are surprised to learn that ritual baptism was practiced in Judaism long before the days of John the Baptist. They may also be surprised to learn that ritual baptism is still practiced today among Orthodox Jews. We tend to think that Christians had invented baptism. But that isn't so.

Baptism originally began as a purification ritual in the days of Moses, but according to Jewish apocrypha, even Adam and Eve immersed themselves in the Euphrates River to symbolize their penitence after being expelled from the garden.

Christians generally have different ideas about how baptism should be done and what it means. Once when I was conducting a Torah class at a small Bible study group, I brought up the issue of baptism. We discussed the Torah origin of the ritual. Everyone was fascinated. Then I asked the students, "From what denomination of Christianity do you each come?" We had three Lutherans, an Evangelical, two Catholics, a Baptist and a Methodist in attendance that night. I said, "Isn't this amazing? We all come from different sects with different ideas about baptism. In fact, this is one of the subjects that divides us the most deeply. But here we are, all learning together about baptism. That's the beauty of discovering our Hebrew roots: Torah is something we all have in common, since it is older than the theologies that divide us now. It is our common origin."

In the days of the Apostles, Jews practiced ritual baptism frequently, sometimes daily. From the days of Moses, all of Israel regularly participated in ritual purification immersions. Anyone who became ritually unclean needed to undergo an immersion before they could enter the Temple. The priests immersed every day. After a woman completed menstruation, she needed to immerse herself before she could rejoin her husband or participate in the Temple. Those who had become contaminated in any way (e.g., lepers) needed to go through immersion before they were deemed ritually pure again. In Judaism, immersions like this are referred to as immersion in a *mikvah*. *Mikvah* is a Hebrew word meaning "gathering of water." A *mikvah* could be a river, a lake, a spring or any naturally fed gathering of water. Ritual immersion in a *mikvah* comprised a regular part of Jewish life.

The Torah forbids anyone from entering into the Temple of God while in a state of ritual impurity, and the only way to be certain of ritual purity is to pass through a *mikvah*.[96] Worshippers going up to the Temple immersed themselves before entering. Modern-day visitors to Jerusalem can see the remains of the *mikvah*s at the foot of the Temple steps. The 3,000 new believers who were baptized on Pentecost in Acts 2 almost certainly were baptized in the *mikvah*s of the Temple Mount. The *mikvah* is a regular feature of Jewish archaeological sites. Immersion baths are found on Masada, at the Herodian, at Qumran and all over the land of Israel.

According to Judaism, a Gentile who wants to become Jewish must undergo several ritual requirements. For men, the two main requirements are circumcision and immersion. For a woman, immersion is the entire conversion ritual. In Jewish thought, a Gentile who converts to Judaism is still a Gentile until he comes up out of the water of the *mikvah*. Going down into the water, the convert is said to die to his old life. As he comes up, he is as a newborn child, a new creature. This immersion into a baptismal pool is the final ritual of conversion. Gentiles who pass through the immersion pool are symbolically said to be reborn as Jews (or 'born again' as Jews, if you prefer).

In Christianity, the symbolism of the baptism is almost identical.[97] Baptism is an important part of discipleship.

REMINDERS

The Torah fills life with daily, weekly, monthly and annual reminders of God. Numbers 15:38–40 refers to one of the daily reminders found in the Torah.

> They shall make for themselves tassels on the corners of their garments throughout their generations…to look at and remember all the commandments of the LORD, so as to do them and not follow after your own heart and your own eyes, after which you played the harlot, so that you may remember to do all My commandments and be holy to your God. (Numbers 15:38–40)

The tassels (*tzitzit*) consist of four sets of knots and strings that hang off the corners of the ritual prayer shawl and a smaller ritual garment worn underneath one's shirt. Even the Master wore the tassels, and they became an important component of His healing ministry.[98]

The commandment of the tassels works in two directions. First, the person wearing the tassels is reminded that he represents God in the world. The tassels symbolize the commandments; by wearing the tassels, a man is accepting responsibility for keeping the commandments. Second, people who see him wearing the tassels are reminded of God. They will hold that individual to a higher level of accountability. The tassels are a conspicuous sign of faith. In that respect, they are similar to the Jesus fish American Christians often put on their cars. Drivers with the Jesus fish on their cars are conspicuous. The symbol reminds them to be more godly on the road, and it reminds other drivers of Jesus.

That's the whole idea of the Torah life. God designed everything in the Torah to remind us of who we are. From the clothes we wear to the food we eat to the days we celebrate—He gave us every law to remind us that we are God's holy and righteous people.

Many of the reminders are explicitly stated as such. For example, the weekly Sabbath is a reminder of the seven days of creation; the Passover is a remembrance of the exodus from Egypt; i.e., a remembrance of salvation and redemption. Other aspects of Torah are not explicitly referred to as 'remembrances,' but together they form a comprehensive lifestyle that never lets us forget who God is or who we are. That's good; we need those reminders. We have a lot to remember!

For example, the Torah tells us that we are to write God's commandments on the doorframes of our houses.[99] Traditional Jews keep this commandment by affixing a small scroll case (*mezuzah*) containing the relevant passage of Scripture onto the doorframes of their homes. It is a clear reminder that the home is a godly home and under the jurisdiction of God's Word. On entering and exiting the home, the observant Jew reverently touches the scroll case to remind him of his obligation to be a godly person inside and outside the home.

Similarly, Moses says we are to bind God's Word to our hands and foreheads.[100] Traditional Jews keep this commandment by strapping leather boxes (*tefillin*) containing relevant passages of Scripture to their hands and foreheads during morning prayer. This ancient custom was universal among the mainstream of observant Jews of Yeshua's day. He almost certainly practiced the custom. Starting each day with a ceremony in which the Word of God is literally strapped to your head and on your arm is a powerful reminder. The daily, weekly, monthly and annual reminders of Torah never give a person an opportunity to forget who they are.

GOD'S COOKBOOK

Another thing that Christianity lost along the way is biblical dietary laws. In the Torah, God gives His people laws about what they can eat and what they cannot eat. These laws are meant to sanctify His people, setting them apart. They are also meant to keep His people healthy, sparing them certain health problems that arise from eating unclean animals.

In Christianity, several key passages of the New Testament have been misunderstood to imply that God's dietary laws no longer apply. These passages are fully explored and explained in other resources.[101] Suffice to say that Yeshua kept the dietary laws, as did all the Apostles. This being the case, we followers of Yeshua should at the very least know something about those laws.

Leviticus 11 distinguishes between two types of animals: the clean (*tahor*) and the unclean (*tamei*). We are commanded not to eat the unclean ones. The distinction between clean and unclean animals did not originate in Leviticus or the Sinai covenant. There is evidence that swine were regarded as unclean by the Babylonians (although they remained on the menu).[102] Noah knew the difference between clean and unclean animals even before the flood.[103] The distinction probably reflects an animal's eligibility for sacrifice. Of those animals that were suitable for sacrifice, seven pairs were taken into the ark. Of those that were not, only one pair was taken.

In the Torah, God considers only mammals that both ruminate (chew the cud) and have a split hoof as permissible for consumption. These animals are characterized as herbivores possessing four stomach compartments and two-toed hooves. Examples include cattle, sheep, goats, buffalo, ibex, gazelle, deer, wild ox and giraffe. Mammals that do not possess these characteristics are regarded as unclean and unsuitable for human consumption.

The Torah permits fish possessing both fins and scales. Other seafood is not permitted. Shrimp, lobsters, clams, oysters and the like are all outside the dietary laws of Torah. Furthermore, many fish are regarded as unclean because they lack fins or proper scales. Whales, sharks, eels and the like are eliminated along with any fish without scales.

As for fowl, the Torah disqualifies birds of prey and carrion. The following birds are regarded as clean in the Bible and/or most Jewish tradition: pigeon, turtle dove, palm dove, hen, chicken, turkey, quail, partridge, peacock, pheasant, sparrow, duck and goose. The ostrich is among the forbidden birds that might commonly be mistaken as food. The eggs of unclean birds are also regarded as unclean.

With the exception of a certain class of locust, the Bible forbids all insects as food.

In addition to these, the Bible forbids the consumption of blood as well as the consumption of meat with the blood still in it (i.e., meat that has not been bled).

First Fruits of Zion's *Holy Cow!*, by Hope Egan, discusses the biblical dietary laws and their natural health benefits. It stands to reason that our Creator would prohibit foods that are not good for our bodies. But there is something deeper to be learned in the biblical dietary laws than just good health sense. The laws of clean and unclean foods teach us about the difference between the permissible and the forbidden, light and dark, right and wrong.

The first prohibition God gave to mankind was a dietary law. Though He permitted man to eat of any other tree in the Garden, He forbade them one tree. The biblical dietary laws bring us back to the garden. They remind us that we are not the authors of morality. God makes the distinctions. It's not a matter of how we feel about a particular thing that makes it wrong or right. A well-cooked pork chop is certainly delicious and desirable, but that doesn't make it permissible. So too with sexual temptations, avarice, and a host of other desirables that flash before our mortal inclinations.

The prophets often used the biblical distinctions between clean and unclean as metaphors for good and evil. Keeping the biblical dietary laws forces us to analyze everything before we put it in our mouths. Does that food have animal products in it? If so, what kind of animal? This basic discipline teaches us to be careful about the things that go into our ears and eyes as well. If we should be careful to avoid eating something that might be deemed levitically unclean, how much more so should we be careful to avoid looking at something spiritually unclean or listening to something unwholesome?

The biblical dietary laws are relevant for believers. At the outset, disciples of the Master might look at Acts 15 where the Apostles mandated a baseline of three dietary laws for the non-Jewish believers coming into the faith. "Abstain from things sacrificed to idols and from blood and from things strangled...if you keep yourselves free from such things, you will do well." (Acts 15:29)

THE BEAUTY OF TORAH LIFE

As Christians, we spend a great deal of effort in our sermons and Bible studies trying to make the Scriptures relevant to us. Perhaps it is time to make our lives relevant to the Scriptures.

When we take on the Master's yoke and begin to walk out the Torah, there is no longer a need to try to make the Bible relevant. Rather than trying to make the Bible fit into our world, our lives begin to fit into the world of the Bible.

The life of Torah is one of quiet beauty and subtle majesty. Until it is experienced, it cannot be understood. Words fall short of explaining. For example, try to explain to someone how your life changed after having met the Master. There are various external things you could relate, but those are only the outward results of something that has happened on the inside. The Christian life is much more than simply changing our behavior. It's about being a new person on the inside, a relationship with God, the filling of the Holy Spirit, and the confidence that comes from being able to call God "Abba."

Similarly, from the outside, the Torah life appears to be a matter of external things; certain holy days, a particular diet, and various laws. But these are only external manifestations of something much deeper.

Throughout the day, week, month and year, the Lord offers a regular rhythm of godliness. The Torah mode of life provides daily prayers and constant reminders. When we arise, we pray. When we eat we bless. When we go in and out, we note the *mezuzah* on the door. His Word is on our lips when we lie down and when we get up and when we sit in our homes and when we go on the way.[104] As the week commences, we mark off the days until Sabbath, eagerly anticipating a day off from work, a day with the family, a day with friends, and a day with the Lord.

Ideally, the Sabbath preparations start on Thursday with extra groceries and dinner plans. On Friday the house is full of activity and good smells. Friday night the soft glow of candles light the table while songs, prayers, blessings, laughter and conversation light up the heart. On Saturday night, we gather with friends to bid the Sabbath farewell and begin the countdown to the next Sabbath.

As the weeks pass, the phases of the moon wax and wane, marking off the biblical months, one after another, marching us toward the appointed times of God's festivals. At Passover season, we clean the house to prepare for Unleavened Bread. Imagine reading to your children on Passover the story of that fateful Passover when the nails pierced our Savior's hands and feet. Imagine annually reliving the Last Supper with a simple Passover meal in your home during which you and your family take the cup and the unleavened bread together in remembrance of the Master. Imagine telling the story of the empty tomb as part of your celebration of the Feast of Unleavened Bread.

Soon we are counting the days until Pentecost. Anticipation grows with each passing day. On the fiftieth day we wake up early to attend the special festival service and hear the Ten Commandments read aloud alongside the story of Acts 2. We are given a small taste of the outpouring of the Spirit. Imagine straining to hear the sound of the Master's trumpet while you listen to the ram's horn trumpet blown on the Feast of Trumpets. Imagine rehearsing the weighty work of Messiah's atonement, confessing your sins in tearful prayers, as you fast through the solemn Day of Atonement.

Five days later, the Feast of Booths finds us in the backyard, building a makeshift hut in which we will eat our meals together throughout the eight days of the festival. Imagine sitting outside in your little booth with family and/or friends, reading together the Gospel story of the Savior's birth, on a cool October evening while the radiant face of the full moon rises over you. Imagine knowing that, in the same way, Yeshua and the Apostles once sat in similar booths on the Mount of Olives during the Feast of Booths under the same full moon. At the conclusion of the Feast of Booths, we start the whole cycle over again. Isn't that how it should be for disciples of Yeshua?

On the other hand, you might feel overwhelmed by all of this. But don't be discouraged. You don't have to try to take on everything all at once. Just take one step at a time. Every step toward God and His Word is a step in the right direction. Rome wasn't built in a day, but it lasted a thousand years.

THE ROAD FROM JERUSALEM

How did we lose all these things?

The New Testament, like any piece of literature, is context-dependent. When we read it outside of its context, it is impossible to accurately interpret its original meaning. Unfortunately for us, shortly after the age of the Apostles came to a close, there was a great schism between believers and Jews. The political upheaval of the First and Second Jewish Revolts coupled with Roman state-sponsored persecution forced non-Jewish believers to disassociate themselves from Judaism. At the same time, believers began to experience concentrated persecution within the synagogues and were actually expelled from participation in the Jewish congregation.

As a result, many Gentile believers in Yeshua were left trying to interpret the Bible with only a superficial knowledge of the original matrix from which it had come. They began to read the New Testament with a decidedly anti-Jewish posture, and interpreted the arguments of the apostolic-age communities as if they were anti-Jewish and anti-Torah arguments. They quickly forgot that Yeshua, the Apostles and all the early believers were Jewish and/or worshipping in a Jewish context.

In the early second century, Marcion the Heretic led a popular uprising within Christianity with the aim of completely removing the Old Testament (and most of the New Testament as well). He wanted a total disassociation from Judaism.[105]

Our early Christian faith took its traditional shape by defining itself in antithesis to Judaism. Therefore, believers began to consider it praiseworthy and meritorious to violate any laws that seemed conspicuously Jewish. Within a few centuries, they began to consider it a service to God to persecute and even torture and kill the Jewish people.

In today's world, the horror of the Nazi Holocaust has shocked us to our senses. We are going back to our Bibles, digging into church history, and researching Jewish sources as we ask ourselves, "How could we have let this happen?" This searching has yielded some surprises. Like archaeologists digging through layers of rubble to find the foundations of the original city, we have begun to clear away years of misinterpretation and anti-Semitic theology. It is exciting work. One of the ancient treasures we have unearthed in this theological, archaeological dig is the Torah itself.

11

THE JOTS AND
TITTLES OF TORAH

KING SOLOMON'S PALACE

We are peering through the lattice of King Solomon's palace. Seated upon the massive throne of ivory and gold with lions and precious stones sits King Solomon himself. The rich smell of cedar panels mingles with the fragrance of perfumes. Our eyes take in silks and delicacies and other things tantalizing to the senses. Around the throne servants hurry and fuss to anticipate every need and whim of the king: Solomon in all of his splendor!

But what is the king doing? Standing before him are two priests holding aloft a scroll of Torah. It is rolled open to the book of Deuteronomy. Spread across Solomon's throne is another roll of parchment over which the king is hunched, pen and ink in hand. He is copying a Torah scroll. He is fulfilling the special commandment of the king to write a copy of the Torah.

The commandment for the king to write a copy of the Torah is found in Deuteronomy 17. By amazing coincidence, Deuteronomy 17 happens to be the chapter of Torah that Solomon is copying as we spy on him. Even now he is beginning to copy the special section of laws that apply to the king.

Therein it is written, "Now it shall come about when he sits on the throne of his kingdom, he shall write for himself a copy of this law on a scroll in the presence of the Levitical priests." (Deuteronomy 17:18) God commands the king to write a copy of the Torah.

This provision is meant to ensure that the king himself submits to the rule of law and does not become a despot without accountability or boundary. Specifically, the passage says that he shall write a copy of the Torah so "that his heart may not be lifted up above his countrymen." (17:20) In other words, the king is subject to the laws of Torah just like everybody else. He has no sovereign exemptions. He has no royal exception or special immunity. By writing a copy of the Torah for himself, the king is reminded that he is not above God's Law. In the eyes of the Torah, the king is just another citizen of God's Kingdom.

THE RULE OF LAW

This basic ethic of Torah is called the Rule of Law. It is similar to the way the constitution of a governing body is meant to function. In theory, a constitution is a document that presides over both the governed and the government. In the constitutional model, ultimate sovereignty is not vested within the government; it is vested in the constitution that formed the government.

This is the theory of modern politics, as is well illustrated in the workings of the United States of America. The Constitution lays out the parameters for American government. Ostensibly, the government is only able to legislate and govern within those parameters. No government official is allowed to overstep the bounds of the Constitution. Government officials are subject to the authority of the Constitution and the legislation spawned by it, just as private citizens are.

Without the Rule of Law, a government would be able to rule capriciously and without mitigation, as is often the case in economies where law has collapsed and violence has prevailed.

In God's economy, the Torah is the constitution that mitigates Israel's government. No one is above God's Torah because no one is above God. His Word is the final authority, and even the king is not to transgress it.

THE SMALLEST LETTER

Knowing this, it is heartwarming to see King Solomon busily engaged in this important commandment. But pay attention. Notice the bored and distracted expressions on the faces of the two priests who are supposed to be checking the king's work. Notice the sweat beading up on the king's forehead. Notice his nervous smile as he glances at the priests and then uses his finger to dab a jot of ink off his scroll. It looks as if King Solomon has just erased a letter from the passage he is copying! The priests overseeing the work don't seem to notice.

The words that the king is supposed to be transcribing are "He shall not multiply wives for himself, or else his heart will turn away." (Deuteronomy 17:17) But what has the king done? He has erased the little letter *yod* (ʾ) from the word *yirbeh* ("multiply"). The *yod* is a letter shaped like an apostrophe and no larger than one. It is just a small jot of ink. But in erasing that letter, Solomon has changed the whole meaning of the sentence. Now it says, "He did not multiply for himself wives and his heart will not turn away." By erasing the letter *yod*, Solomon has changed the tense of the verb "multiply." It is a small and subtle change. But now the verse is no longer an imperative forbidding a king to multiply wives. Instead, it has become a statement implying that his past-tense multiplication of wives will not have the effect of leading his heart astray. Solomon has removed a jot.

AN IMPORTANT MIDRASH

The above scene is more or less described for us in an ancient collection of Jewish teaching called the *Midrash Rabbah*.[106] There we find a crucial teaching that not only relates this anecdote about Solomon, but also informs our reading of the words of the Master in Matthew 5:17–19.

> Do not think that I came to abolish the Law or the Prophets; I did not come to abolish but to fulfill. For truly I say to you, until heaven and earth pass away, not the smallest letter or stroke shall pass from the Law until all is accomplished. Whoever then annuls one of the least of these commandments, and teaches others *to do* the same, shall be called least in the kingdom of heaven; but whoever keeps and teaches *them*, he shall be called great in the kingdom of heaven.

Some expositors try to make these words say something other than what they say. But the *Midrash Rabbah* and Solomon's unscrupulous scribal editing lay the true implications bare. Let's spend some time analyzing this teaching and its relationship to both Deuteronomy 17 and Matthew 5. The first part of the *midrash* is as follows.

> When God gave the Torah to Israel, He gave both positive and negative commands, and He gave some commandments for a king, as it says: "[The King] shall not multiply horses for himself...He shall not multiply wives for himself or else his heart will turn away..." But Solomon arose and studied the reason that God gave this commandment, saying: "Why did God command, 'He shall not multiply wives for himself?' Was it not just to keep his heart from turning away? Well, I will multiply wives and my heart will not turn away." (*Exodus Rabbah* 6:1)

In his great wisdom, Solomon supposed he understood the reasoning behind the commandment. Why did the Torah command a king not to multiply wives? Clearly God intended this law as a safeguard for the king's heart. Solomon apprehended the principle of the law. He understood the intention behind the law against multiplying wives. He thus reasoned, "If I keep my heart from going astray, then I am free to multiply wives." Therefore, he felt at liberty to edit the text of the Torah enough to reflect his new insight into God's Law.

According to this logic, Solomon was able to ignore the command not to multiply wives. In his mind, because he understood the principle of the law, he did not need to obey the literal meaning.

If the wise King Solomon had possessed a copy of 2 Corinthians, as we do, he could have quipped, "The letter kills, but the spirit gives life." No more rationalization would be necessary. In our terms, we could say that Solomon did not need to keep the letter of the law because he understood the spirit of the law.

A Complaint in Heaven

The *midrash* continues with the story of Solomon's edited version of the Torah:

> At that time, the *yod* of the word *yarbeh* went up on high and prostrated itself before God and said, "Master of the Universe! Didn't you say that no letter shall ever be abolished from the Torah? Behold, Solomon has now arisen and abolished one. Who knows? Today he has abolished one letter, tomorrow he will abolish another until the whole Torah will be nullified!" God replied, "Solomon and a thousand like him will pass away, but the smallest tittle will not be erased from thee." (*Exodus Rabbah* 6:1)

According to this story, the little letter *yod* that we saw Solomon blot out from his copy of the Torah was so offended that it ascended to God and filed a formal complaint against Solomon. The letter *yod* warned God that if this kind of editorial process were allowed to continue, the whole Torah would soon be abolished and nullified. God placated that letter *yod* by assuring it that not even the smallest decorative crown would ever be erased from the eternal Torah. He pointed out that Solomon and men like him are temporal and passing, but the Law of God is eternal. Solomon may ply his wisdom and logic and creative scribal work as much as he likes, but God's Law will still stand long after Solomon has disappeared.

Yeshua virtually quoted this *midrash* when He said:

> Do not think that I came to abolish the Law or the Prophets; I did not come to abolish but to fulfill. For truly I say to you, until heaven and earth pass away, not the smallest letter or stroke shall pass from the Law until all is accomplished. Whoever then annuls one of the least of these commandments, and teaches others to do the same, shall be called least in the kingdom of heaven; but whoever keeps and teaches them, he shall be called great in the kingdom of heaven.[107]

CLEANING SEWERS

In the *midrash*, Solomon goes on to explain his rationale. He says, "The reason why God has said, 'He shall not multiply wives for himself' was only lest the king's heart should turn away...God is with me, and I will withstand this temptation."

Solomon is confident that his own wisdom is superior to the rule of Torah. With a terrific sense of irony the *midrash* continues:

> Yet what is written of Solomon? "For it came to pass, when Solomon was old, his wives turned his heart away after other gods" (1 Kings 11:4). Rabbi Shimon bar Yochai said, "It would have been better for Solomon to clean sewers than to have this verse written of him." (*Exodus Rabbah* 6:1)

I spent a good deal of my younger years engaged in the less-than-glamorous vocation of sewer cleaning. So Shimon bar Yochai's words carry extra color for me. The specific color I am thinking of is the black sludge that invariably accompanies a clogged sewer pipe. It never occurred to me as I labored for hour after hour over clogged sinks, tubs and toilets that I was better off than Solomon, but the *midrash* assures me that I was.

In his wisdom, Solomon outsmarted himself. He assumed that because of his rational apprehension of Torah, he was above the Rule of Law. The thinking goes something like this: "I understand what the Torah really meant by such-and-such commandment; therefore, I don't need to actually keep that commandment."

I have often heard pastors explain that the laws of clean and unclean animals that forbade Israel to ingest pork arose because of the absence of refrigeration in the wilderness. Having therefore determined the Torah's reasoning behind the commandment, they claim that we are clearly liberated from keeping this commandment in an age of refrigeration and preservatives.

Again, we might be tempted to explain the law of the Sabbath as God's desire for man to take a break from a heavy workweek. Now, understanding the Torah's intention behind the law of the Sabbath, it becomes clear that we need not keep the Sabbath on the seventh day, as long as we take at least one day off a week.

Furthermore, since it is the Torah's intention that we get the rest we need, if we aren't tired, we don't need to rest and are free from the obligation of Sabbath.

We also find it convenient to spiritualize the commandments. The reasoning might go like this: "I understand the meaning of the Sabbath. It teaches us about the Sabbath rest in Messiah. Therefore I am free from keeping the Sabbath. I may celebrate the Sabbath if I want to, but I don't need to, because I understand that the Torah's purpose is to teach me about the Sabbath rest in Messiah. Since I understand the Torah's intention, I don't need to keep the literal commandment." We have taken our cues from Solomon.

I could go on with endless examples of this kind of rationalization. But we are all familiar with the ingenious arguments we have constructed to exempt ourselves from the Rule of Law. Somehow, even those of us who identify ourselves as Torah-observant seem to find adequate immunity from the Rule of Law when necessary.

Madness and Folly

Regarding Solomon and the unfortunate outcome of his decision to abolish a letter from the Torah, the *midrash* continues:

> For this reason did Solomon say of himself, "I turned to consider wisdom, madness and folly." (Ecclesiastes 2:12) What Solomon meant by these words was this: He said, "Because I tried to be wiser than the Torah and persuaded myself that I knew the intention of the Torah, did this understanding and knowledge turn out to be madness and folly." (*Exodus Rabbah* 6:1)

In the end, Solomon's great wisdom turned out to be madness and folly because he thought he was wiser than the Torah. Through reinterpretation of the Torah, he was able to ignore the Rule of Law. In his estimation, he was above the literal meaning of the commandment because he understood the text at a deeper level. In so doing, his wisdom turned to madness and folly with bitter consequences in his life.

Are believers exempt from the Rule of Law?

It is true that we are not under the Torah as a means of attaining salvation or access to the family of God. The words of Paul are very clear on this point. Grace is by definition a gift. Our salvation is not contingent upon any particular commandment or behavior. Our righteousness is imputed to us, not created by us. There is no magical commandment that when properly observed will suddenly and mystically whisk us from the kingdom of darkness into the Kingdom of Light. Therefore we are not under the law in regard to salvation.

But it would be madness and folly to assume that we are exempt from the Rule of Law, as Solomon did. It would be madness and folly to assume that by merit of our salvation we possess some special immunity to God's commands. It would be madness and folly to cavalierly reinterpret the commandments in such a way as to justify our own disobedience. The rule of God's Law is an eternal ethic.

The Cost of Discipleship

Almost a decade ago, when American President Bill Clinton flouted the Rule of Law regarding his alleged perjury there was a great outcry from conservative Christians. People were incensed that this man considered himself and his office to be above the Constitution and above the criminal court system created by the Constitution. It was called a travesty of justice, and for many weeks the Rule of Law was at the forefront of conversation.

But many of us conservative Christians who condemned the American president for not upholding the rule of American law routinely exempt ourselves from the rule of God's Law. Yeshua anticipated our tendency to absolve ourselves. That is why He reminded us of Solomon's folly when He said, "Do not think that I came to abolish the Torah...not the smallest letter or stroke shall pass from the Torah."

Without ever having read the *midrashic* version of Matthew 5:17–19, Deitrich Bonhoeffer, in his book *The Cost of Discipleship*, incisively explains Yeshua's words regarding the Rule of Law. He writes:

> The law Jesus refers to is the law of the Old Covenant, not a new law, but the same law that He quoted to the rich young man and the lawyer when they wanted to know the revealed will of God. It becomes a new law only because

it is Christ who binds his followers to it. For Christians, therefore, the law is not a 'better law' than that of the Pharisees, but one and same; every letter of it, every jot and tittle, must remain in force and be observed until the end of the world. Jesus has in fact nothing to add to the commandments of God, except this, that He keeps them. He fulfills the law, and He tells us so himself, therefore it must be true. He fulfils the law down to the last iota.[108]

The thing that makes Bonhoeffer so unique among theologians is that he refused to trivialize and explain away the words of the Master. He is one of the few among us who took Yeshua literally. Bonhoeffer did not feel the need to be wiser than Yeshua. He did not try to be smarter than the Gospel. He did not substitute rationalization for obedience. And because of that, Bonhoeffer met martyrdom in the death camps of Nazi Germany while most of his seminary colleagues were goose-stepping around with swastikas on their uniforms. Bonhoeffer believed in the Rule of Law, and to him, a theology that did not confess the Rule of Law was a theology of 'cheap grace.'

The Fundamental Ethic

The Rule of Law is the most basic and fundamental ethic of the Torah. Without the Rule of Law, the ethics of the Torah are reduced to simply good advice, something akin to the fatherly counsel Polonius gives his son Laertes in Hamlet. Without the Rule of Law, the Ten Commandments become the Ten Suggestions.

Yet somehow, we assume that the Rule of Law in Torah does not apply to us. In so doing, we place ourselves even above the kings of Israel. More than that, we place ourselves above Messiah, the ultimate King of Israel.

It is part and parcel of Christian theology that Messiah lived a perfect and sinless life in accordance with Torah law. If He had at any point transgressed Torah, He would have ceased to be the perfect sinless atonement necessary. After all, the Apostles tell us that "Everyone who sins breaks the law; in fact, sin is lawlessness." (1 John 3:4 NIV) Indeed, according to Deuteronomy 17, if Yeshua is a true king of Israel, He must keep Torah "all the days of his life" (vs. 19) and carefully observe "all the words of this law

[Torah]" (vs. 19) and "not turn aside from the commandment, to the right or the left." (vs. 20) Yeshua was not above the Rule of Law, even though He is, in respect to His concealed, divine nature, the author of that law.

I am afraid that our shock at Solomon's devious erasure of the letter *yod* is a little hypocritical. In Christian theology, we have erased whole sentences, verses and chapters of Torah because we have assumed ourselves to be wiser than the Torah. Our wisdom has turned to madness and folly. We have taken our cues from King Solomon rather than from King Yeshua. If that is the case, it would have been better for us to clean sewers than to play at theology.

12

THE DIFFICULT LAWS OF TORAH

"Are you suggesting we go back to making animal sacrifices?" you may ask. "What about the laws of clean and unclean, and stoning adulterers and Sabbath-breakers? Surely you aren't suggesting that, as a part of this restoration, believers should return to these antiquated, harsh and ritualistic laws, are you?

To answer that question, I would like to tell you about Dr. Laura and the Torah.

DEAR ABBY MEETS ELIJAH

A decade or so ago, a voice arose within the American popular culture defending traditional Torah values and norms. At that time, I was working apartment maintenance and often listened to the radio while painting apartments and snaking out sewers. That's when I started listening to Dr. Laura Schlessinger on the radio.

Like the voice of the prophets of old, radio talk-show host Dr. Laura preached a message of repentance across the airwaves. A cross between Dear Abby and Elijah the Prophet, she made a living out of dispensing advice from a conservative Torah perspective. Her candor and remorseless rebukes made her undeniably entertaining, but what was really unusual was her championing of biblical, ethical values and norms in modern culture. She was anything but diplomatic. Her political incorrectness was so shocking and appalling that whenever Dr. Laura attempted to capture a television audience, protests erupted all over the country. The liberal world accused her of being bigoted and homophobic.

Smear campaigns were launched and the protests availed. Advertisers began to pull their sponsorship from the stations carrying her television show. The outcry against Dr. Laura was so great, and her words about morality and decency so insulting that the television networks quickly removed the show or assigned it to an early morning time slot.

Pushing the Hot Button

Was Dr. Laura really a bigot and a homophobe? Probably not. Like many conservative Christians and observant Jews, she simply took a hard stand on morality. She was not willing to accept the popular notion of moral ambiguity. She regarded God's Law as the arbiter of truth, and that entailed a belief in moral absolutes.

But it was not Dr. Laura's defiance of liberal feminism, nor her opposition of day-care parenting, nor her strong pro-life posture that won her the 'most hated conservative' status in American culture. The issue that sank Dr. Laura's ship was her refusal to accept homosexuality as a normal and healthy lifestyle. Standing on the basis of Torah, Dr. Laura declared homosexual behavior to be abnormal.

Her refusal to acquiesce on this issue cost her credibility in the mainstream media, but it won her the love and affection of conservative Christians around the world. The condemnation of the homosexual lifestyle is an issue near and dear to the hearts of conservative Christians everywhere. There are few moral issues that can incite as much passionate vehemence in believers as the gay issue does. Homosexuality has been a 'hot button' in the church for the past two or three decades. Yet despite our rancorous rhetoric against it, the gay agenda has advanced unabated—even within the seminaries of the church itself. Some denominations now officially sanction homosexuality as a viable lifestyle and even perform gay marriages and ordain openly homosexual clergy. The relentless advance of the gay agenda has created such an atmosphere of panic and homophobia in the church that Christians were quick to embrace Dr. Laura as one of our own...even if she was Jewish.

In response to the homosexual movement, conservative Christians are quick to point to specific Torah passages like Leviticus

18:22 in order to justify the hard moral line they are drawing. But according to our own traditional Christian theology, this methodology is flawed.

AN ANONYMOUS LETTER

When the Dr. Laura controversy was at its height, I received the following widely circulated email. It was sent to me by a Jewish believer. He had received it from another believer who was urging him to abandon Torah observance. It continues to circulate on the Internet in different forms. In recent years, it showed up addressed to President George W. Bush. The original version that I received reads as follows:

> Dear Dr. Laura,
>
> Thank you for doing so much to educate people regarding God's Law. When someone tries to defend the homosexual lifestyle, for example, I simply remind him that Leviticus 18:22 clearly states it to be an abomination. End of debate. I do need some advice from you, however, regarding some of the specific laws and how to best follow them.
>
> When I burn a bull on the altar as a sacrifice, I know it creates a pleasing odor for the Lord (Lev. 1:9). The problem is my neighbors. They claim the odor is not pleasing to them. How should I deal with this?
>
> I would like to sell my daughter into slavery, as it suggests in Exodus 21:7. In this day and age, what do you think would be a fair price for her? I also know that I am allowed no contact with a woman while she is in her period of menstrual uncleanliness (Lev. 15:19–24). The problem is, how do I tell? I have tried asking, but most women take offense.
>
> Now I have a neighbor who insists on working on the Sabbath. Exodus 35:2 clearly states he should be put to death. Am I morally obligated to kill him myself? Then, Lev. 25:44 states that I may buy slaves from the nations that are around us. A friend of mine claims that this applies to Mexicans but not Canadians. Can you clarify?

A friend of mine also feels that even though eating shell-fish is an abomination (Lev. 10:10), it is a lesser abomination than homosexuality. I don't agree. Can you settle this? And Lev. 20:20 states that I may not approach the altar of God if I have a defect in my sight. I have to admit that I wear reading glasses. Does my vision have to be 20/20, or is there some wiggle room here?

I know you have studied these things extensively, so I am confident you can help. Thank you again for reminding us that God's Word is eternal and unchanging.

Despite his misapplications and his tendency to violate context, the author of the email to Dr. Laura does make a good case. How can we derive unchanging ethical and moral absolutes from a document we routinely disregard and declare irrelevant to life in the modern world? How can we claim that God's Word is eternal and unchanging while at the same time teach that it has changed?

ABOMINATIONS

In what is certainly his strongest argument, the author of the email compares eating shellfish to homosexuality. Both are described by Torah as abominable to God.[109] The Hebrew word used in both instances is *to'evah*. It is a word used to describe an object that elicits a reaction of disgust and distaste. This word is rarely used in the first four books of Torah, but finds several applications in Deuteronomy. The book of Deuteronomy tells us that God is disgusted by idolatry, child sacrifice, divination, sorcery, witchcraft, spell casting, channeling spirits and consulting the dead. In addition, the Torah says that God is disgusted by the employment of prostitution in worship, gender cross-dressing, remarriage to a previous spouse who has remarried and inaccurate weights and measures used to defraud.[110] In other words, God is disgusted by sin. Whether those particular sins disgust Him more than others is not certain. It should be enough of a deterrent to know that those things disgust the Lord.

In the church I grew up in, all of the above abominations would have received a resounding "Amen!" In fact, we would have been quick to add Leviticus 18:22 to the list. Therein God describes homosexuality as an abomination to the Lord. But our "amen" would have gotten stuck in our throats if we were told that eating unclean animals is also an abomination to the Lord. How do we reconcile condemning homosexuality while going out for the Red Lobster's 'all-the-shrimp-you-can-eat special' on Friday night?

THREE TORAHS OR ONE?

Typically the reconciliation is accomplished by dividing the Torah into three domains of legislation. The Torah seems to contain laws pertaining to morality, laws pertaining to civil government and laws pertaining to ceremony. Based upon these three domains of application, our theologians dice the Torah into moral law, civil law and ceremonial law. We are then able to proceed by saying that the Gospels made the ceremonial laws and civil laws obsolete. Only the moral code remains valid through the new dispensation of grace.

This explanation seems to satisfy the objections of the disillusioned radio listener. His questions regarding the shellfish, Sabbath, sacrifices, priesthood and purity laws can all be dismissed as ceremonial laws long ago shed by the faith. His questions regarding slavery can be dismissed as civil laws, invalidated by the Gospel. Only the moral code remains in force today, which happily includes the prohibition of homosexuality.

The three-fold explanation is, however, flawed at its core and does not withstand modest scrutiny. There are not three Torahs. "There is to be one law [Torah] and one ordinance for you and for the alien who sojourns with you." (Numbers 15:16)

Several years ago, I was invited to teach about Torah at a local Christian Bible school. During the question-and-answer time, one of the students asked, "How can we know if a particular law is moral, civil or ceremonial? The Bible doesn't seem to make any distinction." It is an accurate observation. The distinction between moral, civil and ceremonial laws is artificial and arbitrary. It is a contrivance created for the convenience of popular theology.

At no point does Torah give any indication of a separation between moral and ceremonial law. The ceremonial laws of the prohibition of idolatry and the law of the Sabbath are listed along with the moral statutes regarding murder and theft. The Torah defines eating unclean animals equally abominable as cross-dressing and necromancy. God has not distinguished between ritual laws and ethical laws, but we have.

And because we have, it is possible for some theologians and seminarians to condone homosexuality even in the clergy of the church. Any scriptures condemning such behavior can be readily dismissed as antiquated ceremonial laws, not part of the essential morality of the Bible. Following this line of reasoning, nothing can be said to be absolutely wrong or right. Rather, everything is subject to possible reinterpretation and dismissal as part of the obsolete body of ceremonial legislation.

By dividing the word of God into arbitrary categories, some of which we have declared no longer valid, we have dug our own theological grave and handed the shovel to the opponents of the Gospel. Now we can only shout in protest as they scoop the dirt in on us. The Dr. Laura email is a big scoop of dirt for which conservative Christianity has little answer.

ETERNAL AND UNCHANGING?

The email is a delightfully amusing parody of our misguided handling of Scripture. The anonymous writer astutely observes that we have a double standard when applying Scripture. We only use those passages of Torah that support our moral predispositions. We regard passages that buttress our predispositions as eternal and unchanging. Commandments within Torah that do not support our ethical and religious contrivances, however, are disregarded as obsolete.

To be fair, the writer takes some liberties with the Torah. Most of his points are made from misapplication of specific commandments. He achieves the ridiculous by taking a commandment out of its context and placing it in a different context.

How we choose to respond to his arguments will either make or break our case against homosexuality and every other moral absolute we hope to derive from Scripture. If we allow him to embarrass us into explaining, "Well, those things are ceremonial and cultural things that have been done away with," he will say, "The prohibition against homosexuality is also a ceremonial and cultural issue." We may try to bring in passages from the Pauline scriptures to counter his argument,[111] but these are ultimately futile because Paul derives the authority of his arguments from Torah. If the Torah foundation is malleable, so are the arguments based upon it.

If, however, we maintain that the Torah is unchanging and immutable, as our Master did, we find ourselves on firmer ground. Let's step in for Dr. Laura, President Bush and my Jewish friend by answering the questions.

SACRIFICE

The emailer points out his neighbor's objections to the burnt offering in the backyard. I can empathize with his neighbor. The sacrifices described in Leviticus are only permitted within the Temple and must be facilitated by a Levitically pure priesthood.[112] In the absence of an existing Temple, the rites of sacrifice cannot be practiced. That is not the same as saying that those laws are obsolete or done away with. Yeshua's sacrifice fulfilled the symbolic components of the sacrificial system. But fulfilling and obsolescing are two different things. The book of Acts shows us that the believers remained engaged in the Jerusalem Temple system long after the death and resurrection of the Master.[113] Obviously they did not regard the Temple worship as obsolete.

Ever since the destruction of the Temple in 70 CE, the sacrifices detailed in the Torah have not been possible (and will not be possible) unless (or, better yet, until) God's Temple in Jerusalem is rebuilt. The email author's transference of those laws from their Temple context to the suburban American backyard raises some humorous possibilities, but it is an irrelevant argument.

PURITY

The email author speculates about contact with ritual impurity; namely women in menstruation. Like the laws of sacrifice, the purity laws have a relevant context only when there is a functional Temple. The purity laws of clean and unclean are designed to protect the sanctity of the Temple precinct and priesthood. In the absence of the Temple, the purity laws are only vestiges of a different world. That does not mean the purity laws are obsolete or done away with. If the Temple were rebuilt in Jerusalem tomorrow, every worshipper going to that Temple would be bound by the laws of clean and unclean.

Women in menstruation are only one source of ritual impurity. He selects that particular one because it will incite the strongest reaction. By transferring those laws from their Temple context to Western, postmodern culture, the author of the email again paints a comical scenario, but one that has no real bearing on the Torah's relevance.

PRIESTHOOD

The reference to the defect in eyesight is actually from Leviticus 21:18, not 20:20, but our comedian has overtaxed himself with the reference to 20/20 eyesight and mistaken it for a verse and chapter reference. (Subsequent versions and generations of the email have been corrected.) Regardless of the error, the eyesight law only relates to the priesthood of Israel, and it is a reference to blindness, not astigmatism. It is part of a list of prohibitions that forbid a maimed or disabled priest from facilitating the sacrificial service of the Temple.

Our modern sensitivities and equal-opportunity dogmas are offended by a passage like Leviticus 21:18. Like the sacrifices themselves, the priests handling them needed to be without defect. A priest with a disqualifying defect was still fully employed within the priesthood and had the rights to all venues of the priesthood except the sacred service of the altar.

Still, even if the author of the email had perfect vision and was without any form of physical defect, he would be forbidden to approach the altar unless he is a direct and certifiable descendent of Aaron. There is no wiggle room here. But again, those laws are relevant only when there is a Temple or an altar to approach in the first place.

SLAVERY

The author of the email plays on emotions evoked by our historical memory of American slavery. He claims that Exodus 21:7 suggests a man sell his daughter as a slave. Actually, the passage in question does not suggest this. Rather, it addresses one of the unpleasant possibilities of life in the ancient Near East where a debtor might find himself or family members being taken into slavery in lieu of unpaid debt. The Torah seeks to protect a woman who might be caught in that barbarous system of economics by ensuring her right of redemption and forbidding her resale to another. Thus she cannot be used as a sexual slave, passed from owner to owner. She must be treated with dignity and accorded her rights.

The Torah law he criticizes is actually meant to defend the cause of the slave and the rights of women. Far from being obsolete, it is from Torah laws like this one that the world has learned to treat women with respect and dignity.

He cites Leviticus 25:44 as granting him permission to buy slaves from Mexico or Canada. This time he is correct. The passage he is citing is part of a prohibition on buying Israelites as permanent slaves. The Torah allows fellow Israelites to be purchased only on a temporary basis, and then only as a type of 'hired hand.' After seven years, or at the year of Jubilee, the Israelite slave is released and must be paid for his labor. The same passage does, however, allow for the purchase of heathens as lifelong slaves. Of course, slavery is illegal in Canada, the United States and Mexico, so even if he were to find some heathens for sale in either Canada or Mexico, he would have other legal issues to deal with. He again makes a satirical point by transferring the world of the ancient Near East into Western society. But pointing out that the Torah legislates against permanently subjugating God's people as slaves is not the same as proving that Torah is no longer relevant.

CORPORAL PUNISHMENT

The email author accuses his neighbor of Sabbath violations and wonders about the death penalty associated with the sin. The death penalty assigned to Sabbath-breakers and to other grievous sins of Torah was not a vigilante-style execution as our anonymous author imagines. Those sentences were determined through a court of law employing the adversarial system of justice. If such a court (namely, the Sanhedrin) existed today and had civil jurisdiction in Israel or in the United States, and if the accused Sabbath-breaker was not a heathen, but was demonstrably obligated by Torah to keep the Sabbath, then he would be well advised to get a good lawyer. The anonymous author of our email could stand as a witness for the prosecution in the trial, but a guilty verdict would not be achievable without an additional witness. Also, intention to belligerently break the Sabbath would have to be proven. If all of those criteria were met, then an execution under the auspices of the court would commence.

It strikes us as barbaric and antiquated to imagine someone being stoned to death for breaking the Sabbath. But our self-righteous indignation is the result of our holding the Sabbath in much lower esteem than God does. We have considerably less trouble imagining a court of law putting a murderer to death because that is a reality still present in our cultural milieu. The Sabbath is the most often-repeated positive commandment in the Scripture. It may not seem like a big deal to us, but apparently it is to God.

Unclean Animals

The email author derives his finest point from the eating of unclean animals. Deuteronomy describes it as an abomination to God, just like homosexuality. Yet even the most right-wing conservative Christians enjoy a little lobster tail once in a while. So how can they condemn homosexuality?

We must either acquiesce to the notion that parts of the Torah have been abolished or that we have been wrong about the shellfish and the rest of the biblical dietary laws.

Certainly we could point to several New Testament passages that Christianity has traditionally interpreted as abrogations of the dietary laws, but that would only prove his point about the eternal, unchanging quality of God's Word. If what was called an abomination in one case is now called breakfast, why shouldn't an abomination in another case now be called healthy human sexuality? Hmmm. Food for thought. Or perhaps it's time for a few thoughts about food.[114]

The Difficult Laws of Torah

The Torah contains a plethora of laws that are foreign to us. The laws of the Temple, the sacrificial system and the purity codes are all outside our world of experience. They are only relevant to worshippers entering the Temple in Jerusalem. The laws of punishments and court-imposed sentences seem, at times, unduly harsh because we have grown accustomed to milder systems of jurisprudence. Unfortunately, the criminals in society have as well. But it is important that we do not make arbitrary distinctions, slicing and dicing God's Word in order to make it fit our world view.

We don't make sacrifices today, but only because the Torah forbids us from doing so. Without a Temple and priesthood, sacrificing is a sin.[115] We don't stone Sabbath-breakers today. To do so without proving in a Torah court of law (the Sanhedrin) intentional, flagrant and deliberate violation of a known prohibition (which would be virtually impossible in today's world where the Sabbath is no longer understood or practiced) would be a violation of Torah.

When we encounter difficult laws in the Torah, rather than toss them out, we should take the time to study them. That might require some homework on our part. First Fruits of Zion's *Torah Club* series would be an invaluable help in that effort. *Torah Club Volume Five* lists and discusses all the commandments of the Torah and ranks them according to their applicability, in and out of the land of Israel, with and without a Temple and so on. Some laws apply only to priests. Some apply only to men. Some apply only to women. Some apply only to officers of a Torah court of law. When studying the Torah, it is crucial to examine the context and application of the commandments.

In addition, it is helpful to look at Jewish tradition around a commandment. The Jewish community has more than 3,000 years of experience in handling the Torah and applying its laws. Oftentimes the rabbis see far deeper into the text than our cursory readings allow. They bring a wealth of oral tradition and family history to help clarify difficult passages. Before we go any further, we should take some time out from this discussion to consider the role of Jewish tradition in understanding Torah.

13

THE ORAL TORAH

For purposes of clarity, we have been using a fairly narrow definition of the Torah. We understand the Torah as the five books of Moses: Genesis, Exodus, Leviticus, Numbers and Deuteronomy. However, in traditional Judaism, the five books of Moses are regarded as only part of the Torah. Those books are referred to as the written Torah. In addition to the written Torah, Judaism teaches the authority of an oral Torah. Thus traditional Judaism has two Torahs: the written Torah and the oral Torah.

TWO TORAHS

The oral Torah is a collection of laws, explanations and legal minutia. Allegedly, the Jewish people orally passed these laws on from the days of Moses until the second century CE when they were finally committed to writing. The written code of this vast body of traditional law is called the *Mishnah*. According to the *Mishnah*, God originally gave this additional legislation to Moses, who in turn "transmitted it to Joshua, Joshua to the Elders, the Elders to the Prophets, and the Prophets transmitted it to the Men of the Great Assembly." This quotation from the *Mishnah* (*Pirke Avot* 1:1) attempts to establish an unbroken chain of authority between Moses and the oral Torah. It assumes that the laws and stipulations of the oral Torah originated at Sinai.

The laws contained within the oral Torah are, for the most part, explanations of and expansions on the written Torah's laws. The need for such explanations and expansions is self-evident. The written Torah contains numerous commandments that require more information if they are to be observed. For example, the Torah commands Israel to write the Word of God on the doorframes of their houses and on their gates, but it omits the details of how to accomplish this. What passages of the Scripture are to be written? How are the words to be written on to the doorframes?

These types of details are elements that the written Torah assumes its readership already knows or understands. But that assumption breaks down after thousands of years of separation from the original context. The oral Torah endeavored to preserve those original traditions and pass them on along with the written Torah.

Nine Hundred Years of Bible Study

There are many commandments that require additional information and details. The great medieval Jewish commentator Maimonides points out that while Israel is commanded to build booths and live in them, no instructions are given regarding the specifics of how to build such a booth. In his introduction to the *Talmud*, he writes, "Just as we see that the general principles of [a commandment] were told together with their details and specifics at Sinai, so too, the general principles, details and specifics of all the commandments were told on Sinai." Classical Judaism believes that Moses wrote down the commandments, but passed on the explanations of the commandments orally.

> It should be understood that every commandment that the Holy One, blessed be He, gave to Moses our Teacher, peace unto him, was given to him together with its explanation. God would tell him the commandment, and afterwards He would give its explanation, its substance, and all the wisdom contained within the Torah's verses. (Maimonides' *Mishnah Torah* quoting *Sifra Leviticus* 25:1)

Traditional Judaism, therefore, believes that the oral Torah carries the same authoritative weight that the written Torah carries.

In the early second century, the famous Rabbi Meir began the dizzying task of committing the gigantic body of oral tradition to writing. His work was continued by a wealthy and prominent distant relative of Yeshua named Rabbi Judah the Prince. Judah the Prince completed what Meir had begun. The finished work was a momentous, skeleton-like, written version of laborious legal material called the *Mishnah*. *Mishnah* means "repetition" because, prior to being committed to writing, the material was passed from generation to generation through memorization via repetition. His body of work is commonly called the oral Torah. He completed the work around 200 CE, and it immediately became the textbook of Torah study for world Jewry.

The Sages who lived after the compilation of the *Mishnah* accepted it as the new standard definition of Torah Judaism. In their various schools and academies in Babylon and Israel, they set to work studying and arguing over the *Mishnah*. In their arguments and discussions over the *Mishnah*, the various rabbis told and retold the oral traditions that they had received from their masters. Those traditions were often at odds with the *Mishnah*, resulting in more arguments to try to reconcile with the Torah. In the process, old parables, amusing anecdotes, pieces of antiquated laws, rabbinic proverbs, customs, folklore and superstition were discussed and eventually written down as commentary on the *Mishnah*. The commentary on the *Mishnah* is called *Gemara*, which means "completion" because it adds the oral traditions and proof texts and arguments that the *Mishnah* left out. In that sense, it completes the *Mishnah*.

Two prominent schools of Sages, one in Israel and one in Babylon, independently produced written *Gemara* on the *Mishnah*. In the fourth and fifth centuries, the *Gemara* of Israel's academies was compiled with the *Mishnah* to form the collection called the *Talmud Yerushalami* (*Jerusalem Talmud*). The *Gemara* of the Babylonian academies was compiled with the *Mishnah* to form the even more copious collection called the *Talmud Bavli* (*Babylonian Talmud*). *Talmud* means "study." Both versions of the *Talmud* are the result of 900 consecutive years of Bible study; from the first Sages quoted in the *Mishnah* to the last Sages quoted in the *Gemara*.

Is the Oral Torah Really Torah?

There is a biblical basis for the introduction of additional legislation. Deuteronomy 17:8–13 grants the judges and teachers of Israel the authority to make legal rulings and instructional interpretations based upon the laws of the written Torah. These are meant in the way of clarification and application. Thus, claim the rabbis, the written Torah grants the community leaders in each generation the power to make authoritative and binding decisions regarding how the Torah is to be lived out and practiced. These rulings are also considered oral Torah. Each generation has added to this ever-growing body of legislation.

The problem is not that traditions of men have arisen. We are, after all, men, and any way that we apply a specific commandment is going to be our 'tradition.' The problem is that classical Judaism assumes that the oral Torah (represented by the laws of the *Talmud* and subsequent codifications of those laws) is just as binding and authoritative as the Bible itself. The oral Torah is regarded as equal to the written Torah.

What are believers to do with oral Torah? Admittedly, the concept of an oral tradition does seem to make sense. Much of the oral Torah is ancient and some of the contextual implications it provides could well go back to the generation of Moses. Yet it is far beyond the realm of credibility to suggest that the body of the oral Torah's legislation is all derived directly from Moses. It is not self-evident that all (or even most) rabbinic tradition contained within the oral Torah is derived from Moses and therefore carries the weight of Scripture. On the contrary, the majority of the teachings of the oral Torah are inferences and extrapolations created by the Sages in their attempts to clarify and explain Torah. These elucidations are referred to in Judaism and in the Gospels as the "Traditions of the Elders." When the *Mishnah* was compiled in the late second century and early third century, these traditions were incorporated into the document and thereafter became definitive for Judaism. In the days of Yeshua and the Apostles though, such traditions were just traditions, variously practiced, accepted and argued.

Yeshua Himself lived by and even (through His compliance) endorsed the majority of Jewish tradition. At times, however, He shoved tradition aside. His criteria for doing so were based upon the literal commandments of the written Torah. When a tradition contradicted the written commandments of God, the Master regarded that tradition as void. A classic example of this is the hand-washing question in Mark 7.

EATING BREAD WITH UNWASHED HANDS

In Mark 7, a delegation of Pharisees found Yeshua and His disciples enjoying lunch. The disciples were breaking bread and eating. The Pharisees observed that the disciples had not performed a ritual hand washing before eating.[116]

The custom of a ritual hand washing before handling and eating food belonged to the legislation of the oral Torah, allegedly received from Moses at Mount Sinai. The *Mishnah* dedicates an entire section to the subject of ritual hand washing. Passage after passage considers all the various minutia of the ritual from every conceivable angle. How much water is required? Where can the water be drawn from? What type of water? With what can it be drawn? With what can it be poured? Which hand should be washed first, the left or the right? How much of the hand should be washed? Up to the wrist? Up to the elbow? What if one hand is clean and the other is unclean? And so on.

Despite the detail of this legislation, the requirement to wash one's hands before eating is not a commandment of the written Torah. It is not a command given by God. It is merely a tradition (albeit a tradition that has long since proven valuable in basic hygiene).

The reasoning behind a ritual hand washing before eating can be derived from Torah. In the Torah, human beings can become unclean and even ritually contaminating. For example, someone who has touched a corpse becomes unclean and anyone he touches thereafter will also be rendered unclean.[117] In addition, the Torah specifies that the meat of certain animals is unclean and therefore forbidden for consumption, whereas others are clean and are therefore permissible. In Leviticus 11:32–38 the Torah tells us that otherwise clean food can be rendered unclean if the carcass of certain unclean animals falls onto it.

The oral Torah took these basic biblical concepts and combined them for what would seem to be a logical conclusion. The *Mishnah* teaches that touching bread with unclean hands renders the bread unclean.[118] According to such legislation, an unclean person handling otherwise clean food renders that food unclean and thereby unfit for consumption. Thus if you were unclean (for whatever reason) and went to eat a peanut-butter sandwich with unclean hands, that sandwich would be rendered unclean by your touch. The peanut-butter sandwich would be regarded as unfit for consumption. The *Talmud* says, "Whoever eats bread without first washing his hands is as though he eats unclean food; as it is written, 'In this way the people of Israel will eat defiled food.'"[119]

If that quotation represents the conviction of the Pharisees in Yeshua's day, we can understand their shock and disappointment that Yeshua's disciples did not wash their hands according to the traditions of the elders. They could only regard such an abrogation of the religious norm as a strike against His legitimacy.

But does the Torah really say that bread (or any biblically permissible food) can be made unclean by being handled with unwashed hands? No, it does not.

So they asked Yeshua, "Why don't your disciples walk according to the tradition of the elders?" The Hebrew verb for "walk" (in its root form) is *halach*. The *halacha*, therefore, is the "walking out" of a matter. *Halachah* is the word used to refer to the specific ways in which a person lives out the commandments. An argument over how one is to obey a certain commandment or tradition is called a *halachic* argument. In traditional Judaism, the oral Torah determines one's *halachah*.

The Pharisees were concerned that Yeshua's disciples did not follow the *halachah* according to the tradition of the elders; namely, washing their hands before eating so that the bread wasn't rendered unclean by touch. Yeshua, on the other hand, was unconcerned with ritual hand washing before eating. The ensuing argument between Yeshua and the Pharisees was in essence a *halachic* argument, the likes of which constitute the seemingly endless pages of the *Talmud*.

The Master replied with a quote from Isaiah, with which He declared the ritual hand washing before eating as one of the rules taught by men.

Rightly did Isaiah prophesy of you hypocrites, as it is written: "This people honors Me with their lips, but their heart is far away from Me. But in vain do they worship Me, teaching as doctrines the precepts of men." Neglecting the commandment of God, you hold to the tradition of men. (Mark 7:6–8)

The Pharisaic scruples over hand washing are not commandments of the Torah; they are merely human innovations. Obsession with ritual minutia can serve as a substitute for genuine faith and obedience. Yeshua told the Pharisees that in their pursuit of ritual purity they had let go of the commands of God and were holding on to the traditions of men. He told them they had set aside the commandments of Torah in favor of their own traditions.

But what command of God is being set aside by washing one's hands before eating? It seems like a harmless enough tradition. How does hand washing contradict the command of God?

The Torah commands that we "make a distinction between the unclean and the clean, and between the edible creature and the creature which is not to be eaten." (Leviticus 11:47). By declaring otherwise permissible food to be unclean, simply on the basis that it had been touched by unwashed hands, the Pharisees were transgressing the commandment to correctly distinguish between the unclean and the clean. They were declaring what was clean for consumption to be unclean. They were declaring what was permissible to be forbidden, all on the basis of a tradition. In essence, the commandments of God were being disregarded in favor of a tradition.

THE VALUE OF THE ORAL TORAH

Before we completely throw out the oral Torah and all its 'traditions of men,' we need to point out that Yeshua retained the majority of such traditions. He lived in a Jewish world. He engaged in practices derived from both the written Torah and the oral Torah. He did this deliberately and with intention. For example, before eating, He always blessed God. The written Torah commands us to bless God after we eat.[120] Only in the oral Torah do we learn to bless God before we eat. At His last Passover *seder*, He poured wine and shared it with His disciples, even investing significant Messianic symbolism into that Passover cup. The written Torah, however, says nothing about wine at Passover. Only in the oral Torah do we find the tradition of serving cups of wine as one of the elements of the Passover s*eder* meal. Numerous other examples could be cited, but a careful reading of the Gospels makes it clear—Yeshua kept and endorsed a great deal of traditional law.

His participation in such matters of Torah was not accidental. It was not simply because He happened to live in a Jewish culture that He kept some Jewish traditions. Rather, He was the Torah made flesh. He was here to show us all how to do Torah, and He seemed to have no qualms about challenging traditions of which He did not approve.

The oral Torah is a valuable piece of the Torah heritage and should not be dismissed simply on the basis that it is largely traditional. However, Yeshua clearly did not regard the oral Torah as an authority on par with the written Word of God. Neither should we.

YESHUA AND THE ORAL TORAH

In His day, Yeshua saw the direction the Tradition of the Elders was going, and He battled for leniency. He endeavored to demonstrate that compassion and human dignity take precedence over legal stringencies. When He went to heal the blind man, He spit in the dirt and mixed the spittle with the dirt to make mud, even though it was the Sabbath. He used the mud to heal the man on the Sabbath. When He healed the cripple, He told him to pick up his mat and carry it. All of those acts—even healing itself on the Sabbath day—were violations of the stricter schools of oral tradition. His disciples didn't wash their hands before eating bread, they husked grain in their hands on Sabbath, and so on. All of these stories are told to show us Yeshua arguing for a more just and accurate application of Torah.

With regard to Himself and His own approach to Torah, He said:

> Come to Me, all who are weary and heavy-laden, and I will give you rest. Take My yoke upon you and learn from Me, for I am gentle and humble in heart, and you will find

rest for your souls. For My yoke is easy and My burden is light. (Matthew 11:28–30)

In Jewish literature, the yoke is a common metaphor used to refer to the Torah; specifically the application of Torah.[121] A yoke is the mechanism that applies the strength of an ox to a plow. So too the yoke of Torah is the application of Torah in one's everyday life. In another passage, Yeshua uses similar language to criticize the Pharisees and teachers of Torah who had made the practical observance of Torah difficult by adding layers of stringency, additional legislation and minutia to the commandments of God. He said, "[The Pharisees] tie up heavy burdens and lay them on men's shoulders, but they themselves are unwilling to move them with *so much as* a finger." (Matthew 23:4) That's how He characterized the stringencies of the emerging oral Torah: binding and tying heavy burdens. The cumulative result of centuries of tradition, law after law and additional derived stringencies, was a heavy yoke that made practical observance of the Torah a virtual impossibility.[122] To those who are wearied and burdened by the quagmire of legal minutia, Yeshua offers a simpler and clearer approach to Torah. His yoke is easy. His burden is light.

Yet at the same time, we see that Yeshua lived by the normative oral traditions of Judaism. This is obvious from the things He did, the things His disciples did and the traditions the believers kept. Listen to what He said: "The scribes and the Pharisees have seated themselves in the chair of Moses; therefore all that they tell you, do and observe." (Matthew 23:2–3)[123] On the one hand, He argues against some of the oral traditions; on the other hand, He endorses them.

Isn't that a contradiction?

No, it is not. In the days of Yeshua, the oral Torah was not yet codified. It would be more than a century before Rabbi Judah compiled the *Mishnah*, five centuries before the completion of the *Talmud*. In the days of the Master, the oral Torah was still emerging. Thus we see Yeshua arguing the specifics of how to apply Torah just like the Sages of the *Mishnah* and the *Talmud* argued with one another. In a typical Talmudic argument, Rabbi So-and-So forbids something, but Rabbi Such-and-Such permits it. These arguments constitute most of the oral Torah. Yeshua, in the Gospels, fits well into that context, arguing with the Sages just like the famous Rabbi Hillel argued with Rabbi Shammai.

Modern disciples should not simply adopt the whole oral Torah as it exists today, because our Master didn't. He objected to certain aspects of it. On the other hand, we cannot just throw out the whole oral Torah, because our Master didn't. He kept a great deal of it. Is there a solution to this contradiction?

The Easy Yoke

Jewish tradition and Jewish thought are a rich part of the Torah heritage, but they are not our source of identity, nor are they a substitute for obedience to the Word. Some commandments are difficult to obey or understand without the help of tradition; however, many people get caught up and distracted in outward expressions.

The Apostolic Scriptures give us two primary tools for determining the value and legitimacy of any given tradition. Be it a Jewish or Christian tradition, before we incorporate it into our faith and practice, we should test it against these two principles.

1. Don't Break the Commandments of God

> Yeshua asked the Pharisees, "Why do you break the commandments of God for the sake of your tradition?" (Mark 7:8) The guiding principal we learn here is that the written Torah (the Word of God) always trumps the oral Torah (the traditions of men). If a certain tradition or stringency contradicts Scripture, we must discard it.

> For example, the oral Torah forbids playing musical instruments on the Sabbath. However, the written Torah commands the blowing of trumpets on the Feast of Trumpets. In traditional Judaism, when the Feast of Trumpets falls on a Sabbath, the trumpets are not blown. Thus the commandment of God (to blow a trumpet on the Feast of Trumpets) has been broken for the sake of a tradition (to not play a musical instrument on the Sabbath).

2. Don't Go Beyond What Is Written.

In 1 Corinthians 4:6, Paul urges us "not to exceed what is written, so that no one of you will become arrogant in behalf of one against the other." This seems to have been a dictum of the early believing community. What does it mean to "exceed what is written"? It means that if one cannot find a biblical basis for a particular tradition, it is irrelevant to the legitimate application of a biblical life.

Jewish tradition forbids playing musical instruments on the Sabbath. Yet nowhere in the Scripture will one find a prohibition on playing musical instruments. It is a stringency that has gone beyond what is written. It is a prohibition superfluous to the real application of Torah.

The tradition of lighting Sabbath candles before dark on Friday nights does not contradict the Word of God. Neither does it go beyond what is written, because it is part of honoring the Sabbath, sanctifying the Sabbath and keeping the Sabbath holy. Traditional Judaism safeguards the biblical prohibition against lighting a flame on the Sabbath by lighting lamps before the Sabbath.[124] Therefore it has a good biblical footing. If a person found candle lighting to be a meaningful part of welcoming the Sabbath, he or she should do so in full confidence. The steady flame of the Sabbath candles can bring warmth to homes and hearts as we celebrate the Light of the World.

On the other hand, the tradition of lighting Sabbath candles sometimes becomes an end in and of itself. I have often seen Sabbath candles lit well after the Sabbath has begun in order to keep the tradition. Once again, the commandment of God (not to light a fire on the Sabbath) is set aside for the sake of tradition.

When we turn to Jewish tradition, we should remember that it is not Torah, on the same level as the Word of God, and it is subject to the above two-fold criteria.

This is the easy yoke of Yeshua—the pure, simple commands of God, unburdened by piles of legal tradition. As the Apostle John said, "For this is the love of God, that we keep His commandments; and His commandments are not burdensome." (1 John 5:3)

THE LIVING TORAH

Having offered the above cautions, it seems appropriate to remember what Torah really is. It is the instruction of God. It is the covenant between God and His people, renewed through Yeshua the Messiah. It is likened unto the wedding vows between a husband and wife. It is the Word, the will and the wisdom of God. It is the tutor that leads us to Messiah.

As we approach Torah and Jewish tradition, we must remember that the goal of Torah is Messiah, not Jewish expression. As long as we keep our eyes firmly upon the Living Torah, we will be able to find an appropriate balance of the written Torah and the oral tradition. We need look no further than Yeshua.

As disciples of the Master, we are imitators of Yeshua. He is our oral tradition. His ways form our *halachah*. It is enough for the student to be like his Teacher.

14

PAUL AND TORAH

A few years ago, I was lecturing at a local evangelical seminary when the dean of the school sensed that there was something amiss with my teaching. He requested a meeting with me. In his office, the dean asked about my view of Torah. He was perplexed by my belief that the commandments of Torah are relevant to Christians. I was not explicitly teaching this in the seminary classes, but word got around.

I explained my position on the matter. I explained that in the Bible, Yeshua and His followers were all Torah-observant. They kept the Sabbath. They kept the festivals. They kept the dietary laws. As an aspiring disciple of Yeshua, I felt that it made sense to do the same.

He listened carefully and politely. When I finished, he explained his position on the matter. "You are right," he conceded, "that James the brother of Jesus and the twelve disciples were Jews who continued to practice Judaism. But that is because they did not understand what Jesus was trying to do. That's why the Holy Spirit raised up Paul to take the Christian faith out from under the law. The Jewish Christians in Jerusalem misunderstood. They missed the movement of the Spirit."

I was astounded. "So you are suggesting that Jesus' brothers and His disciples didn't get it? They missed the boat?" He affirmed that this was indeed his belief. The suggestion then is that Yeshua's efforts on the twelve were wasted. After three years of teaching them and leading them, they still did not understand grace. They had misunderstood what God was doing. Even the brother of

Yeshua had missed the point. God had to raise up Paul to remedy their sad devotion to their ancient religion.

It is a staggering proposition, and one that I cannot seriously entertain.

But what about Paul? Didn't Saul the Pharisee convert to Christianity, change his name to Paul, forsake the Torah, and teach freedom from the law? No. He did not.

It is time to take a good, hard look at the Apostle Paul—from his original Torah perspective.

THE PAUL OF ACTS

When we meet Paul in the book of Acts, he is a Pharisee and a student of Gamaliel, the man who defended the Apostles before the Sanhedrin. He is a Greek-speaking Jew from Tarsus. His Hebrew name is Shaul (Saul); his Greek name is Paul. Contrary to popular Christian legend, Yeshua did not change his name from Saul to Paul. Instead, it was common among Diaspora Jews to have a Hebrew name and a Greek name. The same custom is common even today among the Jewish people. When among Greek speakers he used his Greek name, Paul.

Paul never abandoned the Torah. He was a Torah-observant Jew until the day he died. His enemies claimed otherwise. False rumors were circulated regarding Paul.

The book of Acts tells us that when Paul came to Jerusalem after many years of spreading the Gospel among the Gentiles, he met with James the brother of Yeshua and the other elders of the community—the survivors among the Master's original disciples. James presided over the Jerusalem council of elders. He was a man so devoutly Torah-observant that he was called "the Righteous" even by non-believing Jews. The original disciples of Yeshua and the ultra-observant brother of Yeshua voiced their concerns regarding Paul's ministry to the Gentiles. They had heard the rumors that Paul was teaching against Torah, but they were not willing to believe such slander.

Nonetheless, the Jerusalem elders were concerned about the slander, not because they suspected Paul of actually teaching against Torah, but because they wanted to clear his name among the believers.

And they said to him, "You see, brother, how many thousands there are among the Jews of those who have believed, and they are all zealous for the Law [Torah]; and they have been told about you, that you are teaching all the Jews who are among the Gentiles to forsake Moses, telling them not to circumcise their children nor to walk according to the customs. What, then, is *to be done*? They will certainly hear that you have come." (Acts 21:20–22)

According to James and the elders, three specific allegations had been raised against Paul.

1. He was teaching Jews to turn away from Torah. (Moses = Torah)

2. He was teaching Jews not to circumcise their children.

3. He was teaching Jews not to live according to the customs.

It is ironic that most Christian theologians have accepted these false allegations as gospel truth. In their zeal to believe that Paul taught against the Torah, they naturally want to believe that the accusations were founded in the actual teachings of Paul. According to Christianity's traditional view of Paul, they are quick to agree. "Of course Paul taught against Torah, against circumcision and against Jewish customs."

But he did not. His opponents and adversaries were misconstruing his inclusion of and leniency toward the new Gentile believers as an anti-Torah posture. James and the Jerusalem elders had already endorsed that leniency[125] and understood the rumors about Paul to be patently false. They said, "All will know that there is nothing to the things which they have been told about you, but that you yourself also walk orderly, keeping the Law [Torah]." (Acts 21:24) They rejected the notion that Paul was not Torah-obedient. Had Paul been anything other than a Torah-observant Jew, he should have seized the moment to correct the Jerusalem elders. He did not. Instead, he consented to their plan to demonstrate to all of Jerusalem that he was, indeed, Torah-observant.

Whose Side Are We On?

It is alarming that Christians have refused to accept the testimony of Paul, James, the elders of the Jerusalem assembly and the book of Acts. Instead we have, for centuries, clung to the idea that Paul taught against Torah and lived a Torahless life as a Christian. It makes me wonder whose side we are on.

The difficulty facing the Jerusalem elders about Paul was in regard to the other believers. When the believers heard that Paul was in town, they would certainly demand a formal inquiry into the allegations. Therefore the council chose to act preemptively by suggesting that Paul join several believing Nazarites in a purification ceremony to fulfill their Nazarite vows, and underwrite the expenses himself. They felt that such a magnanimous and pro-Torah act would disprove the allegations.

Paul had undertaken a Nazarite vow years earlier when leaving Corinth,[126] and now that he was in Jerusalem, that vow needed to be completed or reinstituted. To do so for himself and for others would be considerably expensive. Multiple Temple sacrifices were required. (You can read about the Nazarite temple rituals in Numbers 6.) Rather than protest, Paul consented to the plan. He wanted to demonstrate to the believers that the rumors were false and that he was walking in obedience to the Torah.

Paul's Own Testimony

Throughout the book of Acts, Paul continues to plead his case, protesting his innocence and insisting that he had remained faithful to Torah. To the mob that assaulted him in the Temple he declared, "I am a Jew, born in Tarsus of Cilicia, but brought up in this city, educated under Gamaliel, strictly according to the law [Torah] of our fathers, being zealous for God just as you all are today." (22:3) When standing before the Sanhedrin he asserted, "I have lived my life with a perfectly good conscience before God up to this day." (23:1) To the Sanhedrin, such a statement could only mean, "I have walked according to Torah." He went on to tell them, "Brethren, I am a Pharisee, a son of Pharisees." (23:6) Notice the present tense. He did not say, "I was a Pharisee." He said, "I am a Pharisee."

Before Felix, he testified to "believing everything that is in accordance with the Law [Torah] and that is written in the Prophets." (24:14) Before Festus, Paul protested, "I have committed no offense either against the Law [Torah] of the Jews or against the temple." (25:8) Before Agrippa and Bernice he argued, "All Jews know my manner of life from my youth up...[until imprisonment] I lived *as* a Pharisee according to the strictest sect of our religion." (26:4–5) He went on to say, "I stand to this day testifying both to small and great, stating nothing but what the Prophets and Moses said." (26:22) Finally, in his appeal to the Jewish leadership of Rome, he said, "Brethren...I had done nothing against our people or the customs of our fathers." (28:17) If Paul was faithful to keep even the oral Torah, the "customs of our fathers," how much more so did he keep the written Torah?

For us to suppose that Paul was anything less than scrupulously Torah-observant is to deny the testimony of James, the testimony of the Jerusalem elders, the testimony of Luke (the author of Acts) and the testimony of Paul himself.

In His Own Words

Paul's own words on the subject indicate his high regard for Torah. Consider the following passages pulled from Paul's epistles:

◊ For it is not the hearers of the Law [Torah] who are just before God, but the doers of the Law [Torah] will be justified. (Romans 2:13)

◊ If the uncircumcised man keeps the requirements of the Law [Torah], will not his uncircumcision be regarded as circumcision? And he who is physically uncircumcised, if he keeps the Law [Torah], will he not judge you who though having the letter *of the Law [Torah]* and circumcision are a transgressor of the Law [Torah]? (Romans 2:26–27)

◊ Do we then nullify the Law [Torah] through faith? May it never be! On the contrary, we establish the Law [Torah]. (Romans 3:31)

◊ So then, the Law [Torah] is holy, and the commandment is holy and righteous and good. (Romans 7:12)

◊ For we know that the Law [Torah] is spiritual. (Romans 7:14)

◊ For I joyfully concur with the law [Torah] of God in the inner man. (Romans 7:22)

◊ Messiah is the end [goal][127] of the Law [Torah]. (Romans 10:4)

◊ *What matters is* the keeping of the commandments of God. (1 Corinthians 7:19)

◊ Therefore the Law [Torah] has become our tutor *to lead us* to Messiah, so that we may be justified by faith. (Galatians 3:24)

◊ For by grace you have been saved through faith; and that not of yourselves, *it is* the gift of God; not as a result of works [of Torah], so that no one may boast. For we are His workmanship, created in Messiah Yeshua for good works [of Torah],[128] which God prepared beforehand so that we would walk in them. (Ephesians 2:8–10)

◊ We know that the Law [Torah] is good, if one uses it lawfully. (1 Timothy 1:8)

◊ Keep the commandment [Torah][129] without stain or reproach. (1 Timothy 6:14)

◊ All Scripture is inspired by God and profitable for teaching, for reproof, for correction, for training in righteousness; so that the man of God may be adequate, equipped for every good work [of Torah].[130] (2 Timothy 3:16–17)

These are not the words of a man who turned his back on God's Torah.

Paul's Argument

Why is it, then, that so many Pauline passages seem to disparage the Torah and even encourage us not to keep the Torah? The problem is one of context.

From our perspective it is almost impossible to read Paul in context. We live in a day when the majority of Christians do not keep the particulars of Torah (such as Sabbath, festivals, dietary laws, etc.). Therefore, when we read Paul's letters, his arguments often seem to be anti-Jewish and anti-Torah in defense of modern Christianity. But Paul did not live in our day. He never knew modern Christianity or even the Christianity of the second-century Church Fathers. In Paul's day, believers were part of the larger Jewish community. The seventh-day Sabbath was still the regular day of worship. The believers were still meeting in the synagogues. "For Moses from ancient generations has in every city those who preach him, since he is read in the synagogues every Sabbath." (Acts 15:21) Paul's letters must be understood in this larger Torah context.

It is important to remember when reading Paul's letters, that we are reading only one side of an argument. The Apostle Paul found himself locked in a long-term argument with other Jewish believers over the role and position of non-Jews in the Kingdom of Heaven. His opponents asserted that before a Gentile could be saved, he must first be circumcised (which in Paul's day meant a conversion to Judaism) and keep the whole Torah of Moses. "It is necessary to circumcise them and to direct them to observe the Law of Moses," they said. (Acts 15:5) Paul regarded these requirements, which they regarded as necessary for salvation, as an insult to the grace afforded in Messiah.

As I explain in *The Mystery of the Gospel* (FFOZ, 2003), from Paul's vantage, for a Gentile believer to become circumcised under the auspices of a 'conversion' to Judaism was redundant. It was an affront to Messiah because it implied that faith in Him was not adequate to secure a position in the covenant with Israel. It was a denial of the Gospel. Paul said, "If you let yourselves be circumcised [that is, undergo a formal conversion into Judaism as a necessary component of your salvation], Messiah will be of no value to you at all." (Galatians 5:2 NIV) Messiah is of no value because the convert has opted to accomplish his participation in Israel through his own physical efforts. To Paul's way of thinking, ritual conversion after salvation was like campaigning for an office for which you had already been elected.

In Galatians, Paul responded to his opponents' teaching by forbidding the Galatians to circumcise. He may have even gone so far as to discourage all Gentile believers from circumcision as long as the commandment of circumcision was being misunderstood as a means for acquiring salvation.[131] In the case of Gentiles with Jewish heritage, however, Paul did not hesitate to circumcise. In fact, he personally oversaw Timothy's circumcision. Gentiles like

Titus[132] or the Galatians, he encouraged to remain uncircumcised so long as circumcision was understood as the ticket into the Kingdom. (These matters are discussed more extensively in other works available through First Fruits of Zion.)

In addition, Paul argued vociferously against requiring non-Jewish believers to adopt the stringencies of rabbinic interpretation. The early believers were split into two camps. Some insisted on yoking Gentile believers with the whole body of traditional oral Law and custom, and some resisted that attempt. In Paul's letters, argumentation on this issue can be observed in conflicts over conversion, circumcision, food contaminated by idols and even Sabbaths and festivals.[133]

If Paul ever did command his non-Jewish readers to "remember and observe the Sabbath, keeping it holy," or any other external aspect of Torah, his words would have been used as ammunition by those who were in favor of requiring the Gentiles to observe a stricter, more traditional Jewish lifestyle. Instead, Paul avoided the controversy over the particulars by following the Master's lead in emphasizing matters of character, morality and right living. The only ritual issue he contended over is that of the requirement of circumcising Gentiles as a token of conversion to Judaism.

When read outside the context of this argument, though, we are apt to misunderstand Paul completely. When we forget that he was arguing against requiring Gentiles to be circumcised in order to merit salvation, we are apt to suppose that he was arguing against keeping Torah. But he was only arguing that Torah and circumcision could not be regarded as prerequisites for salvation.

PAUL AND THE DISCIPLES OF YESHUA

In the Great Commission, Yeshua commanded His disciples to make disciples of all Gentiles and to teach them to obey everything He had commanded them. He said, "Go therefore and make disciples of all the nations...teaching them to observe all that I commanded you." (Matthew 28:19–20) Though Paul was not one of the twelve disciples who originally heard this commission, he certainly took up that mantle of discipleship and the commission of apostleship. Any discussion of Paul's attitude toward Torah must factor in his radical discipleship to Yeshua.

The Apostle Paul told the Corinthians, "Be imitators of me, just as I also am of Messiah. Now I praise you because you remember me in everything and hold firmly to the traditions, just as I delivered them to you." (1 Corinthians 11:1–2) In his second letter to the Thessalonians he warned the believers to stay away from those who had abandoned the oral traditions that he had taught and modeled while with them.

> Now we command you, brethren, in the name of our Lord Yeshua the Messiah, that you keep away from every brother who leads an unruly life and not according to the tradition which you received from us. For you yourselves know how you ought to follow our example, because we did not act in an undisciplined manner among you. (2 Thessalonians 3:6–7)

The tradition Paul taught was a life of imitation of Yeshua. It was discipleship at its simplest. Disciples are more than just converts! They are beholden to the expectations of discipleship. "A pupil is not above his teacher; but everyone, after he has been fully trained, will be like his teacher." (Luke 6:40)

Yeshua's Great Commission is more than just proselytism; it is a command to raise up disciples in the name of the Master who will walk in the ways of the Master, learning His words, carrying on His traditions and raising up more disciples for Him. Paul accomplished this. He continually exhorted his converts to walk in imitation of him as he imitated Messiah.

You have probably heard the proverb "What's good for the goose is good for the gander." I call Paul's brand of radical discipleship the Goose-Gander Model. We are the ganders, and the Master is our Goose. Whatever Yeshua said and whatever He did is good enough for us. We are to be imitators of Messiah.

This model is a powerful argument for living a life of Torah. Did Yeshua keep the commandments? Obviously he did. If it's good for the goose; it's good for the gander. Did He keep the Sabbath, the Passover, and the biblical dietary laws? It is all part of discipleship. If we are His disciples, we are obligated to imitate Yeshua. And that is the simple rationale for a Gentile believer to live out the Torah life.

In the Great Commission, Gentile disciples are directed to obey everything Yeshua commanded the twelve. Among those commands is the command to keep the Torah—every jot and tittle of it.[134] Paul certainly knew this and lived by it.

Thus the call to the Kingdom is a call to the Torah of Yeshua. Discipleship is a call to imitation and obedience. Like Paul, we are called to be disciples of Yeshua, and as such it is our job to imitate Him, obey Him and raise up more disciples for Him. The Sabbath, the festivals, the calendar, the dietary laws and all the laws of Torah are components of imitation and obedience in that regard.

> This is how we know we are in him: whoever claims to live
> in him must walk as Yeshua did. (1 John 2:5–6 NIV)

Paul knew Yeshua and walked as He walked. Surely he encouraged his students to do likewise.

Paul, Man of Torahlessness?

Paul is regularly accused of disposing of the Torah. Most traditional Christian theologians would agree that he was a man of 'Torahlessness.' A careful, contextual reading of his writings, however, reveals just the opposite.

Paul was a Torah-keeper. Paul's pro-Torah convictions are evident from his warnings to the Thessalonians regarding the rise of the Antichrist. Paul referred to the Antichrist as the "Man of Torahlessness." In Matthew 24, Yeshua predicted a coming time of apostasy. He said, "Many false prophets will arise and will mislead many. Because lawlessness [Torahlessness] is increased, most people's love will grow cold." (Matthew 24:11–12)

Paul echoed the same warning to the Thessalonians when he said:

> [The end] *will not come* unless the apostasy comes first,
> and the man of lawlessness [Torahlessness] is revealed,
> the son of destruction, who opposes and exalts himself
> above every so-called god or object of worship, so that
> he takes his seat in the temple of God, displaying himself
> as being God. Do you not remember that while I was still
> with you, I was telling you these things? The mystery of
> lawlessness [Torahlessness] is already at work; only he
> who now restrains *will do so* until he is taken out of the

way. Then that lawless [Torahless] one will be revealed… the one whose coming is in accord with the activity of Satan, with all power and signs and false wonders, and with all the deception of wickedness." (2 Thessalonians 2:3–10)

Far from being a man of Torahlessness, Paul warns us against the Man of Torahlessness—the Antichrist, who will perform signs and wonders. The main criteria Paul gives us for recognizing this imposter is that he will be opposed to the Torah of God. Torah is the measure we are given to distinguish a false prophet from a real prophet and a false messiah from the real Messiah. However, Paul lamented that even in his own day Antichrist's spirit of Torahlessness was already at work. If it was so in Paul's day, how much more so in our own?

Paul in Context

In order to read Paul in context, we must remember that Paul was a Torah-observant Jew throughout his life. He was writing to believers who were already congregating in the synagogue and participating in the Torah life. He was locked in an argument over the inclusion of Gentile believers in the faith. His opponents insisted that Gentiles could not be saved unless they first became Jewish. If we fail to remember these points, we will inevitably misunderstand his letters. After all, his letters contain "some things hard to understand, which the untaught and unstable distort, as *they do* also the rest of the Scriptures, to their own destruction." (2 Peter 3:16)

If it was easy to misunderstand Paul in Peter's day, how much more so in our own day? For that reason, we must resist becoming impatient or irritated with brothers and sisters who read and understand Paul differently than we do.

To assist in reading Paul in his original context, the ministry of First Fruits of Zion has produced several resources, such as Tim Hegg's *The Letter Writer* (a thorough introduction to Paul and his world), *The Mystery of the Gospel* (an exploration of Paul's theological posture regarding non-Jews) and *Torah Club Volume Five* (where Paul's comments on the Torah and the commandments are carefully considered).

15

ResTorahation

Confessions of a Judaizer

I believe that God is restoring His people in our day. He has begun by returning the Jewish people to their ancient homeland. At the same time, He is returning His Torah to the disciples of Yeshua.

But from my perspective, there is more at stake than prophetic destiny. I am concerned for the reputation of Yeshua and the integrity of our faith in Him. I love our faith and our Messiah. I teach and write about the Torah in defense of the legitimacy of our hope in Messiah. I believe that without the restoration of Torah, we risk discrediting Messiah. Let me explain.

In Deuteronomy 13, Moses warned Israel about false prophets. Most people who claim to be prophets are not. Generally, this is self-evident. A false prophet may predict something that fails to transpire, or produce a sign or wonder that fails to signify anything wondrous. According to Moses, such a prophet has "spoken presumptuously" and is to be put to death.[135]

Even if the would-be prophet's sign or wonder does succeed and his prediction comes to pass, he might still be a false prophet. Signs and wonders are not the final proof. If the prophet attempts to dissuade Israel "from the way in which the Lord your God commanded you to walk," (13:5) we are to disregard him as a false prophet. The way in which God commanded Israel to walk is the Torah and its commandments. Deuteronomy warns us that we must not listen to such a prophet, even if his ministry comes with amazing signs and wonders. Instead, we are to "follow the Lord... keep His commandments, listen to His voice." (13:4)

These details are easily overlooked because the example Moses uses in Deuteronomy 13:2 is that of a prophet who counsels us to follow after other gods. Yet the enticement to idolatry is just one example of what a false prophet might say to contradict Torah. Moses goes on to make it clear that all the commandments are in view. If the would-be prophet counsels us to break the commandments, he must be deemed a false prophet. For example, an alleged prophet who declared that God had sanctioned an adulterous relationship can be immediately identified as a false prophet because He has contradicted Torah. God cannot contradict Himself.

Moses says that a false prophet might be allowed to perform signs and wonders in order to test Israel's fidelity to Torah. The Master warns us that "false prophets will arise and will show great signs and wonders." (Matthew 24:24)

IS JESUS A FALSE PROPHET?

According to God's own criteria for determining a false prophet, Judaism's rejection of the traditional Christian Jesus is a matter of obedience. Not only is it justifiable, it is a commandment of the Bible. The traditional understanding and presentation of the Christian Jesus is that He was a prophet (and more), attested by signs and wonders, but that He also cancelled the Torah. Such a person fits Deuteronomy 13's description of a false prophet perfectly. Conversion to faith in such a person would be a violation of God's own commandments. It is worthwhile to note that the *Talmud* accuses Yeshua of this very crime, of enticing Israel to idolatry. Deuteronomy 13:9 is adduced as the grounds for His execution.[136]

Yet the real Yeshua of the Gospels is not such. He has little affinity with our traditional portrayal of Jesus. He is a prophet (and more) attested to by signs and miracles, who called Israel to submit their lives to the highest standards of Torah. His message was a call to repentance. This explains why His opponents among the Judean leadership labored so hard to find some way of demonstrating that He was a breaker of Torah. If they could prove that He was teaching against Torah, they could invalidate

His claims. They were unable to do so. Nevertheless, Christianity has consistently presented Him as a prophet teaching against the Torah. A messiah who breaks Torah and teaches others to do so is no messiah at all.

An anecdote from Jewish-Christian dialogue illustrates this point well.[137]

Christian leaders in Czarist Russia held debates in which they attempted to persuade the Jewish community to accept Jesus as Messiah. At one point, they listed all the signs, wonders and miracles that Jesus performed in the Gospels as evidence of Messianic claims. One of the elders of the Jewish community asked, "Are not the teachings of the Nazarene based upon the Torah of Moses?" When the missionaries conceded that they were, the rabbi said, "Our Torah unequivocally and clearly prohibits us from abolishing any commandment of the Torah at the behest of a prophet who performs miracles. It says, 'You shall not listen to the words of that prophet...for the Lord your God is testing you.'" (Deuteronomy 13:3)

In our presentation of the Gospel to the Jewish people, we have consistently invited them to throw off the Torah and follow the Messiah. According to the Bible's own criteria, we thereby disqualify Him as prophet and Messiah. Our presentation is self-defeating and discredits Messiah and His message. We bring shame on the Gospel.

If the Word of God is true, it must be consistent. If Messiah is true, He must be consistent with the Torah of Moses. The Messiah of the Gospels is consistent with the Torah, but the Christ of traditional theology is not. It is my desire to see the Gospel restored. Just as the Jewish people are being restored to the land of Israel, I hope to see the message of the Gospel restored to Torah. That is why I am passionate about returning the Gospel to its original context. I am not a legalist, nor am I a Judaizer. I am a believer, and I believe that our faith is worth defending. If we have made mistakes, let's own up to them and move on.

DESTROYED FOR LACK OF KNOWLEDGE

In a sense, the Gospel has been in exile since the days of the Apostles. Like the Jewish people sent into exile, the Gospel was dispersed among the Gentiles. Like the Jewish people wandering far from home, the Gospel has been far removed from its Jewish context. Like the Jewish people undergoing assimilation among the nations, the Gospel has suffered the effects of syncretism among the nations. Today, the exile is coming to an end.

In ancient Israel, neglect of the Torah led to idolatry, apostasy and exile. In the days of kings and prophets, neglect of the Torah brought the kingdom of Judah to the brink of disaster, "for they have rejected the law [Torah] of the Lord of hosts and despised the word of the Holy One of Israel." (Isaiah 5:24)

Israel and Judah went into exile for turning away from the Torah. "They have not listened to My words, and as for my law [Torah], they have rejected it also." (Jeremiah 6:19) "Me they have forsaken and have not kept My law [Torah]." (Jeremiah 16:11) "Nor have they feared nor walked in My law [Torah] or My statutes...Therefore...Behold, I am going to set My face against you for woe, even to cut off all Judah." (Jeremiah 44:10–11) "My people are destroyed for lack of knowledge. Because you have rejected knowledge, I also will reject you...Since you have forgotten the law [Torah] of your God, I also will forget your children." (Hosea 4:6)

The Temple was destroyed because the people transgressed the Torah. "Like an eagle *the enemy comes* against the house of the Lord, because they have transgressed My covenant and rebelled against My law [Torah]." (Hosea 8:1) "If you will not listen to Me, to walk in My law [Torah] which I have set before you...then I will make this house like Shiloh, and this city I will make a curse to all the nations of the earth." (Jeremiah 26:4–6)

If turning away from the Torah inflicted the wound, then returning to Torah is the balm.

AT THE VERY LEAST

Not everyone will share my theological convictions. Not everyone who reads this book will come to the same conclusions. But at the very least, I hope we can begin to reorient the way we think about Messiah and Torah. We should agree to read the Gospels and the Epistles from a Hebraic perspective. We should agree that the true Yeshua from Nazareth is a Jew who lived a pious Jewish life, in full accord with the commandments of God.

Within the believing Torah movement today, there is a healthy debate about the relationship non-Jews should have with the Torah of Moses. It is my conviction and the belief of First Fruits of Zion, that the Torah is applicable to all Israel, not just those who are native born, but also those who have been grafted into the greater commonwealth of Israel.

Others may disagree with this position, but I hope we can all agree that God's chosen people Israel have not been replaced, and neither has His Holy Torah been abolished. If we can begin to move past the old theological slogans and recognize that Israel is still God's people and the Torah is still His law, then we have come a long way already. The nightmares of our history and the atrocities of our historic anti-Semitism can be left in the past. We need not carry them into the future.

The Restoration

In the church today, one often hears the mantra, "God is doing a new thing." This catchphrase is usually offered to explain the latest popular fad or charismatic wave to wash up on the shallow shores of modern religious expression. I believe that God is doing an old thing. God, who never changes, is pouring out the same message He has always delivered through His holy prophets; "Return to My Torah. Obey My commandments." This is the restoration Moses spoke of in Deuteronomy 30 when He said, "And you shall again obey the Lord, and observe all His commandments which I command you today." (30:8)

Around the world, spontaneously and simultaneously, believers are rediscovering the Torah. They are asking questions. They are seeking answers. They are knocking at the ancient gates. Though Torah-keeping believers largely vanished from the earth shortly after the days of the Apostles, our own generation has seen an amazing rebirth among the disciples of Yeshua. For the first time in almost 2,000 years, believers are taking on the Master's easy yoke. It is not a matter of legalism or heavy bondage; it is a matter of love.

> He who has My commandments and keeps them is the one who loves Me; and he who loves Me will be loved by

My Father, and I will love him and will disclose Myself to him. (John 14:21)

I believe that in these last days, God is preparing a remnant of believers who will walk and live according to His commandments. The Apostle John tells us that in the last days there will be a remnant of believers who will stand against the Antichrist. They are those "who keep the commandments of God and hold to the testimony of Yeshua." (Revelation 12:17) If God is to fulfill this prophecy, He must first raise up a remnant of believers who keep the commandments of God.

Inspired by the Holy Spirit, many believers in Messiah, Jewish and Gentile alike, are feeling a deep longing to return to the biblically observant lifestyle founded in the Torah. Why? The Scriptures say:

> Now it will come about that in the last days...many peoples will come and say, "Come, let us go up to the mountain of the LORD, to the house of the God of Jacob; that He may teach us concerning His ways, and that we may walk in His paths." For the law [Torah] will go forth from Zion, and the word of the Lord from Jerusalem. (Isaiah 2:2–3)

As the world continues to grope in the darkness, men and women from all walks of life are heeding this call of the Spirit to return to the faith established thousands of years ago. Far from being some new, innovative fad, the return to Torah is a restoration of something very old. Through the prophet Jeremiah, the Lord has declared, "Stand by the ways and see and ask for the ancient paths, where the good way is, and walk in it; and you will find rest for your souls." (Jeremiah 6:16) The ancient paths are the paths of Torah. The good way is the way of the Master, the way of discipleship. For He has declared, "Take My yoke upon you and learn from Me, for I am gentle and humble in heart, and you will find rest for your souls. For My yoke is easy and My burden is light." (Matthew 11:29–30)

APPENDIX

THE TORAH CLUB

Now Go and Study

We have in our possession the words of an ancient scroll. Though largely shunned in traditional Christian interpretation, these words form the foundation on which our knowledge of God is built. They are the words of Genesis, Exodus, Leviticus, Numbers and Deuteronomy—the five books of Moses. Collectively they are called the Torah, the instruction of God. They are the most sacred texts of Judaism and the foundation on which the Gospels and Apostolic writings stand. They are the biblical heritage. They are the substance of Messiah.

Ask your heart, "Is it time to unroll the scroll?"

The *Talmud* says that there are things for which a person receives reward, both in this world and in the world to come. They include acts of charity, donations to the work of God, participation in the festivals, deeds of loving-kindness, but "the study of Torah is equivalent to them all."[138] The study of Torah is considered the highest form of service to God because it leads to obedience in all other areas. If the Torah really is God's will and wisdom, His direction and instructions, His unchanging eternal law, and His agent to lead us to Messiah, then we are obligated to invest time and energy in learning it.

The study of Torah is the study of God, for He is the giver of the Torah. It is the study of Messiah, for He is the essence of the Torah. As such, it is an exalted form of worship, a means by which we can intersect the holy.

If you are one of the many believers who are hearing this divine call and are longing for the ways of Yeshua, First Fruits of Zion is pleased to offer you a gateway to Torah. The *Torah Club* presents a unique opportunity to study the Torah in depth, from Genesis to Deuteronomy.

THE TORAH READING CYCLE

When at last God brought restoration and return from captivity, Ezra and Nehemiah and the men of their generation set to work creating a system to encourage Torah study. They wanted to ensure that the people would not slip into idolatry again. They created the synagogue system in which the people heard the Torah read every week.

To this day, the Jewish world studies a weekly portion of the Torah every Sabbath. Jews read the Torah aloud in synagogues on Sabbaths, Mondays and Thursdays. Monday and Thursday are the ancient market days. The market brought the rural people into town on Mondays and Thursdays where they had the opportunity to hear the Torah. On Sabbath days the people assembled according to the commandment.

Since the days of the Apostles, the Torah continues to be read every week in the same manner.[139] An annual lectionary, the Torah reading cycle, allows all Israel to study the same passages of Scripture as they work through the Torah from week to week. The lectionary divides the Torah into two- to six-chapter readings for each week. Corresponding readings from the Prophets are tacked on to the weekly Torah readings. The Torah reading cycle begins in the fall, after the Feast of Tabernacles, with Genesis 1:1. Twelve months later it concludes with the end of Deuteronomy.

Reading along with the weekly Torah readings is a great way to study through the Torah every year. When you do, you are studying in synchronization with all Israel. Synagogues and study halls and Messianic congregations all over the world are studying the same passages of Scripture along with you.

WHAT IS TORAH CLUB?

Unlike other Bible study programs that try to 'figure out' what the Bible is about from our modern, Western world view, the *Torah Club* program returns students to the ancient landscape of Hebraic-Jewish thought. Rather than forcing disparate Bible passages to fit together, the *Torah Club* puts the whole puzzle together naturally and easily.

Torah Club is a five-year, Messianic, Torah study program designed around the weekly Bible portions. In addition to learning the deep wisdom of the five books of Moses (Vol. 1), *Torah Club* students will learn to find Yeshua in the Torah (Vol. 2), study selected passages and stories from the Prophets (Vol. 3), and methodically work through the Gospels and Acts (Vol. 4) to understand how all Scripture connects to form a cohesive whole. In the last year of the program, *Torah Club* students learn how the words of Torah informed the Epistles of Paul and can be applied to their own lives (Vol. 5). Thus the *Torah Club* study program reaches across the whole of Scripture, a Bible study of the whole Bible.

Year One	Volume One	Unrolling the Scroll	Biblical Living in Today's World
Year Two	Volume Two	Shadows of the Messiah	Discovering Messiah in Torah
Year Three	Volume Three	The *Haftarah*	The Prophets
Year Four	Volume Four	The Gospel of Messiah	Commentary on the Gospels and Acts
Year Five	Volume Five	Rejoicing of the Torah	The Epistles and the Life of Torah

Once a month, students receive a packet of study materials. Bible reading assignments are accompanied by copious written commentaries. The commentaries include insights from ancient Jewish Sages, modern Messianic and non-Messianic rabbis and cutting-edge evangelical scholars. Notes and citations invite students to delve deeper into the original sources. Study questions formatted for individuals and/or small groups make the *Torah Club* a perfect curriculum for Bible school students, home school students or congregational cell groups and home fellowships. Additionally, *Torah Club* students receive weekly audio CDs with further teachings and insights on the weekly portion.

But that's not all. *Torah Club* students also have the option of receiving Hebrew language textbooks and Hebrew lessons on the audio CDs. Think of learning to read the words of Moses in their original language! And there's more. *Torah Club* students also have on-line support from the staff of First Fruits of Zion. Questions about Torah, Bible study, faith and observance can be submitted in the *Torah Club* discussion forum at www.ffoz.org and will be answered and discussed by Torah teachers from First Fruits of Zion. *Torah Club* students from all over the world are able to post their discussion points on the weekly materials, transforming their computers into a virtual *yeshiva* (rabbinical seminary) and *beit midrash* (house of study).

Each volume of the *Torah Club* series provides one year's worth of study materials. Those materials will enrich your relationship with God and His Word for the rest of your life. Though it is not necessary, we encourage students to begin with Volume One in their first year and stick with the program until its conclusion. Like a Bible school education, each year is progressive, building on truths and lessons established in previous volumes. For students completing all five years of the *Torah Club*, First Fruits of Zion will issue a 'diploma' of Torah which can be displayed in the office, study or home.

Torah Club teaches things that are not taught in Sunday school. For example:

◊ The complete consistency of 'Old' and 'New Testament'

◊ The continuing relevance of God's laws for believers

◊ The truth of the biblical Sabbath and festivals

◊ The true identity of God's eternal chosen people

◊ The significance of the believer's relationship to Israel

◊ The call to personal and community holiness

◊ The practical application of the commandments in the modern world

◊ The principles of discipleship.

Torah Club invites you to worship God in a disciplined, practical study of the Word every week. But we do not want to study just for the purpose of study. Rather, we study to learn, and we learn to do. The study of Torah is meant to result in good deeds, living lives that are holy, pleasing and acceptable to God. *Torah Club* teaches students how to avoid the traps of legalism while learning to walk out the commands of God. *Torah Club* will not only change the way you think about the Bible, it will change the way you think!

TREASURES NEW AND OLD

Yeshua once told His disciples, "Every teacher of the law [Torah] who has been instructed about the kingdom of heaven is like the owner of a house who brings out of his storeroom new treasures as well as old." (Matthew 13:52 NIV)

The greatest value every *Torah Club* student receives is a thorough education in God's eternal Word. But in addition to those treasures of eternal value, subscribing *Torah Club* members also receive a great deal of value now.

If you were to compile all the sources necessary for recreating the teachings of the five years of *Torah Club*, it would take a library of hundreds of books costing thousands of dollars. Each *Torah Club* volume is like a digest of commentary and thought culled from rabbinic and evangelical sources. More than just a one-time study program, your *Torah Club* materials will become reference works that you will consult again and again as you continue to study God's Word.

Torah Club membership includes the following:

◊ Weekly Bible reading schedules from synagogue lections

◊ Extensive written Bible commentary from rabbis and evangelical teachers

◊ Accurate documentation of original sources

◊ Study questions for home school and small-group discussions

◊ Fifty-two weekly audio CDs with Torah commentary and teaching

◊ High-quality, attractive binders for written and audio materials

◊ Free subscription to First Fruits of Zion's *messiah magazine*

◊ Hebrew language lesson option

◊ Online support and Q&A

◊ Virtual community fellowship with other *Torah Club* students

◊ Discounts on FFOZ products and conferences.

Torah Club is not only a great value and asset for every member; it is also the primary source of revenue for the First Fruits of Zion ministry. *Torah Club* members receive a tax-deductible receipt for more than 70 percent of their total subscription price. Each *Torah Club* member can enjoy the fact that their subscription is supporting a balanced, biblically sound ministry that is dedicated to proclaiming the Torah and its way of life, fully centered on the Messiah, to today's people of God.

Five Volumes of Torah Club

There are five volumes of *Torah Club*—five years' worth of intensive study materials. Each volume takes a different approach or discusses a different section of the Scriptures.

Torah Club Volume One: Unrolling the Scroll

This new volume of *Torah Club* is unlike any Bible study you've ever done; it is Torah 101 for everyone. Every sincere believer desires to live a committed, rewarding life submitted to God's Word. This introduction to the Torah provides new, yet refreshingly ancient insights into the Bible Jesus read. Drawing from Judaism and the Hebrew Roots of Christianity, students will uncover a lost heritage that points toward the paths of godliness. *Torah Club Volume One* is rich with new insights and practical implications, which exhort students to practice righteousness while developing a deeper relationship with our Father in Heaven.

Torah Club Volume Two: Shadows of the Messiah

The name says it all: "Shadows of the Messiah!" The second volume of *Torah Club* lifts the veil and reveals the person of Messiah within the Torah. Yeshua Himself declared, "Here I am—it is written about me in the volume of the scroll..." (Hebrews 10:5–7 NIV). Employing a wealth of the ancient rabbinic and modern Messianic thought on the weekly Torah portions, Volume Two is like walking the Emmaus Road with the Master Himself, where, "beginning with Moses and with all the prophets, He explained to them the things concerning Himself in all the Scriptures." (Luke 24:27)

Torah Club Volume Three: The Prophets

Let the Torah be your gateway to the rest of the Hebrew Scriptures. Volume Three takes students into selected readings from the books of the prophets that accompany the weekly Torah portions. Students will learn the stories, characters, situations and scenarios surrounding the prophets of Israel. Rediscover the vanished world of kings and prophets as the Torah leads you through the history of ancient Israel. Meet characters like David, Elijah, Hezekiah, Isaiah and Jeremiah. Decode the difficult words of the prophets. The spirit of prophecy will water your soul as you peer into the coming Messianic Kingdom.

Torah Club Volume Four: The Good News of Messiah

Torah Club Volume Four takes students on a passage-by-passage study through the Gospels and the book of Acts. It is a commentary that allows the Gospels to be studied from within the context of Torah and classical Judaism. These materials make the leap and repair the breach between the Torah of Moses and the Gospel of Messiah. Club members will see Yeshua and His world in vivid new strokes and colors that will fire the heart. Eye opening—Volume Four is like reading the Gospels for the very first time.

Torah Club Volume Five: The Rejoicing of the Torah

Standing on the shoulders of Volumes One through Four, *Torah Club Volume Five* incorporates the themes of Torah, Messiah, Prophets and Gospels laid down in the previous volumes, but does not repeat that material. Instead it rejoins the annual Torah cycle for an exhilarating dance through the narratives, poetry and laws of the books of Moses while pulling in relevant material from the Apostolic writings and the Epistles of Paul. Volume Five lists out and explains each of the commandments of Torah. Questions of practical application are addressed along with the difficult Pauline passages. Volume Five brings all the Scriptures together in a celebration of spirit and truth.

From Torah Study to Torah Community

The Apostle Paul tells us to "Give attention to the public reading of Scripture, to exhortation and teaching. Do not neglect the spiritual gift within you…" (1 Timothy 4:13–14)

At First Fruits of Zion, we are often contacted by people from around the world who are seeking fellowship with like-minded believers. They are looking for faith communities where the whole Word of God is studied and lived out. They are seeking Torah communities and wondering how to begin them.

We have found that such communities cannot be fabricated or artificially created. Formulas used for 'church plants' usually fail to create successful Torah congregations. Before a congregation is even considered, you need a committed fellowship of believers who are working through God's Word together in a disciplined manner. The *Torah Club* offers a venue for that to happen.

Torah Club offers small-group members a special package discount price. All the students in your small group agree to read and study the materials. Then you meet together once a week and discuss the study questions. Discover the joy of learning while you teach! *Torah Club* provides a forum for in-depth study of God's Word, which naturally lends itself to the development of community and the implementation of God's commandments. It's a great way to introduce people to their rich biblical heritage and a great forum to grow into a Torah community.

As your community continues to grow, First Fruits of Zion is here to provide the additional materials you will need to transition from weekly study group to community.

Torah Club is a great place to begin your renewed journey with Messiah.

BIBLIOGRAPHY

Ante-Nicene Father's Volumes 1-4. Christian Classics Ethereal Library, 2001.

Berkowitz, Ariel and D'vorah. *Torah Rediscovered*. First Fruits of Zion, 1996.

Bonhoeffer, Deitrich. *The Cost of Discipleship*. Collier Books. Mac-Millan Publishing, 1959.

Cohen, Abraham. *Everyman's Talmud*. Schocken Books, 1975.

Chrysostom, John. *Eight Homilies Against the Jews (Adversus Judaeos)*. [Online at www.fordham.edu/halsall/source/chrysostom-jews6.html]

Edersheim, Alfred. *Jesus the Messiah*. Hendrickson Publishers, 1993.

Egan, Hope. *Holy Cow! Does God Care About What We Eat?* First Fruits of Zion, 2005.

First Fruits of Zion. *Torah Club*. Five Volumes. First Fruits of Zion.

Hegg, Tim. *The Letter Writer, Paul's Background and Torah Perspective*. First Fruits of Zion, 2002.

Hegg, Tim. *It is Often Said, Comments and Comparisons of Evangelical Thought & Hebraic Theology*. 2 Vols. First Fruits of Zion, 2003.

Hegg, Tim. *Fellow Heirs, Jews and Gentiles Together in the Family of God*. First Fruits of Zion, 2003.

Kaplan, Aryeh. *The Aryeh Kaplan Anthology Vol 2 (Waters of Eden)*. Mesorah Publications Ltd., 1995.

Lachs, Samuel Tobias. *A Rabbinic Commentary on the New Testament*. Ktav Publishing House Inc., 1987.

Lancaster, D. Thomas. *Mystery of the Gospel*. First Fruits of Zion, 2003.

Lewis, C. S. *The Abolition of Man..* Harper Collins, New York, 1974.

Lewis, C. S. *Mere Christianity*. Harper Collins, New York, 1980.

Moseley, Ron. *Yeshua: A Guide to the Real Jesus and the Original Church*. Messianic Jewish Publishers, 1996.

O'Quinn, Chris. "Fiscus Judaicus," *Bikurei Tzion*, #72. First Fruits of Zion.

Patai, Raphael. *The Messiah Texts*. Wayne State University Press, 1988.

Weissman, Moshe. *The Midrash Says, Shemos*. Bnai Yaakov Publications, 1995.

Whiston, William. *The New Complete Works of Josephus*. Kregel Publications, 1999.

Williamson, G. A. *Eusebius, The History of the Church*. Mpls, MN. Augsburg Publishing, 1965.

The Soncino Talmud. Brooklyn, NY. Judaica Press.

The Soncino Midrash Rabbah. Brooklyn, NY. Judaica Press.

Encyclopedia Judaica. Keter Publishing, 1972.

Weiner, Peter F. *Martin Luther, Hitler's Spiritual Ancestor*. Hutchinson & Co. Ltd. [Online at www.tentmaker.org/books/MartinLuther-HitlersSpiritualAncestor.html#jews]

Scripture Reference Index

Genesis

1:1...166

Exodus

6:7...34
20:2...34
21:7..................................125, 130
23:5...61
35:2...125

Leviticus

1:9...125
10:10...126
11:32–38......................................139
11:47..141
15:19–24......................................125
16:30..95
18:22..................................125, 126
19:18..43
19:28..11
20:20...126
21:18...130
23:2..90
23:2–44..98
25:44..................................125, 131

Numbers

15:16...127
15:38–40......................................105

Deuteronomy

4:5–8..63
6:4–5..77

13...159
13:2...160
13:3...161
13:4...160
13:5...159
13:9...160
17:17...115
17:18...113
17:19...121
17:20...114
17:8–13..138
18:15..2
22:2-3..75
24:14–15..69
30:3–5..1
30:8........................2, 13, 28, 163

1 Kings

11:4...118

Psalm

19:7..30

Ecclesiates

2:12...119

Isaiah

2:2–3...164
5:24...162
56:6–7..86
66:23..80

Jeremiah

6:16...164

6:19..162
16:11..162
26:4–6..162
31:33..............................33, 63, 73
44:10–11....................................162

Hosea

4:6...162
8:1...162

Zechariah

14:16..96

Matthew

5:17..31
5:17–19.............................. 115, 120
5:19..39
7:12..39
11:28..79
11:28–30............................. 85, 143
11:29–30...................................164
12:34..61
13:52..169
22:40..40
23:2–3..143
23:4..143
24:10–12......................................21
24:11–12....................................156
24:24..160
24:31..95
24:9–12..77
26:18..91
28:19–20....................................154

Mark

2:27..85
7..139
7:6–8..141
7:8..144

Luke

4:16......................................47, 48
4:20..48
6:40..................................... x, 155

6:5.......................................78, 85
21:20–22......................................15
22:15–16......................................92
22:19..91
23:54–56......................................85
24:27..171

John

1:14..97
1:17..73
1:2..72
3:16–17..45
5:19..85
8:10..44
8:11......................................42, 44
8:5..42
8:7..44
8:9..44
9:16..82
14:21..164
14:27..79
16:2..16
18:31..42
19:30..81

Acts

15:21..153
15:29..108
15:5..153
20:19–30......................................21
20:7..83
21:20–22....................................149
21:24..149
22:3..150
23:1..150
23:6..150
24:14..151
25:8..151
26:22..151
26:4–5..151
28:17..151

Romans

2:13..151

2:14–15..............................59
2:26–27............................151
3:23...........................30, 35
3:31...........................x, 151
6:3–4..............................71
7:12...............................151
7:14...............................151
7:22...............................152
10:4..........................30, 152
13:8–10...........................40

1 Corinthians

4:6................................145
5:7–8..............................91
7:19..............................152
11:1–2............................155
15:20..............................93

2 Corinthians

3:14...............................33
13:5...............................71

Galatians

3:24..........................31, 152
5:14...............................40
5:2...............................153

Ephesians

2:8–10........................x, 152
2:8–9........................10, 11
3:17...............................71

Colossians

1:27...............................71
2:16–17............................97

2 Thessalonians

2:3, 7.............................22
2:3–10............................157
3:6–7.............................155

1 Timothy

1:8...............................152
4:13–14...........................172
6:14..............................152

2 Timothy

3:16–17.......................49, 152

Hebrews

4:9–10.............................80
8:10...............................33
10:5–7............................170

James

1:22–25............................68

2 Peter

3:8................................79
3:16..............................157

1 John

2:4–5..............................41
2:5–6.............................156
3:4..........................30, 121
5:1–5..............................x
5:3..........................78, 146

Revelation

12:17.............................164

Subject Index

A

abomination, 125, 126, 132
adultery, 40
  woman caught in, 42, 43
Anabaptists, 25
ancient paths, 2
anti-Semitism, 16, 26, 163

B

baptism, 76, 102, 103, 104, 105
Barnabas, epistle of, 18
Bar Kokba, 17
Bible
  and the Protestants, 24
  and the reformation, 22, 23
  God's teaching, 32
  Jesus', 47, 48, 49, 50
  Marcion's, 19
  parts of, 51
Builder's cubit, 37, 38, 45

C

Calendar
  God's, 89, 98, 103
Church
  anti-Jewish sentiment, 17, 22
  replaced the Jews, 17
  Roman, 20
  separating from Judaism, 16
Church Fathers, 10, 18, 73
  and Judaizers, 10, 21
  attest to Torah-keeping
    believers, 78

Ignatius, 18
John Chrysostom, 21
Justin Martyr, 19
circumcision, 10, 14, 104, 149,
    151, 153, 154
Constantine, 20
Council
  of Antioch, 20
  of Jerusalem elders, 148, 150
  of Laodicea, 20
  of Nicea, 20
Covenant, 50, 72, 86, 146, 162
  earlier and later, 52
  the new, 63, 73
  the old and the new, 32, 33

D

Dark Ages, 22
Day of Atonement, 90, 94, 95,
    98, 110
Dead Sea Scrolls, 26
Diaspora, 13
dietary laws, 14, 78, 98, 106,
    108, 147, 155, 156
  and the Church Fathers, 21
  unclean animals, 107, 127,
    132
discipleship, 99, 105, 154, 155,
    156, 164
  cost of, 120

E

Easter, 20, 24

exile, 162
  of the Gospel, *13, 14, 22, 27,*
    161
  of the Jewish people, *25, 161*

F

false prophet(s), 21, 52, 54, 77,
    156, 157, 159, 160
Feast of Booths, 90, 96, 98, 110
Feast of Trumpets, 90, 94, 98,
    110, 144
festivals, 90, 98, 99, 101, 154,
    156, 165
  and the Church Fathers, *19,*
    20, 21
  and the Protestants, *24*
  biblical, *8, 10, 14*
  shadows of Messiah, *97*
  sighting of the moon, *102, 109*
first century, 50, 72
First Fruits, 92, 93
  of the Barley Harvest, *92, 98*
Fiscus Judaicus, 16

G

Gemara, 137
Gentiles, 10
  and circumcision, *154*
  and table fellowship, *10*
  and the Law, *59*
  hearing the Gospel, *148*
  inclusion of, *15, 18*
  will hear Torah, *86*
goal
  of Torah, *30, 146, 152*
Great Commission, 154, 155,
    156

H

heretic, 16
  Marcion, *19, 111*
Holocaust, 6, 26, 27, 111
homosexuality, 124, 126, 128,
    132

I

Institute of Holy Land Stud-
    ies, 6
Israel
  fellow heirs with, *15*
  lost sheep of, *14*
  Messiah, king of, *121*
  non-Jews grafted into, *14, 71*
  return from exile, *161*
  salvation of, *35*
  Scriptures of, *14*
  sent into exile, *162*
  the commonwealth of, *163*
  the covenant with, *32, 33*
  the land of, *13, 27, 76*
  the people of, *13, 25, 34, 58*
  the State of, *27*

J

Jerusalem
  destruction of, *15, 16, 17, 85*
  Temple, *76, 129, 132*
Jewish tradition, 34, 94, 133,
    138, 140, 142, 145, 146
Jewish Wars, 15, 16, 77, 111
Jews
  persecution of, *17, 18, 24, 77*
jot and tittle, 121, 156
Judaism, 83, 103, 136, 140, 143,
    145, 147, 160, 165
  and Christianity, *14*
  conversion to, *99, 104, 153,*
    154
  inclusion of Gentiles, *15*
  Messianic, *8*
  separating from, *16, 19, 20,*
    111
Judaizer, 9, 10, 21, 24, 159

K

ketubah, 34, 35. *See*
    also Covenant

L

Laura Schlessinger, 123
law. *See* Torah
  Gk. nomos, 29
Legalist, 11
Levitical
  priesthood, 129
  priests, 113
levitical
  cleansing, 102
Luther, 23, 24, 25, 26

M

Marcion, 19, 111
Messiah
  believer's identity in, 71
  dwells in believers, 71
  false, 157, 161
  festivals, shadows of, 97
  goal of Torah, 30, 152
  King of Israel, 121
  Living Torah, 146
  Lord of the Sabbath, 82
  resurrection of, 20, 93
  sinless life, 121
  Word made flesh, 72
mezuzah, 106, 109, 136
midrash, 9, 115, 116, 119
mikvah, 104. *See also* baptism
Mishnah, 135, 137, 138, 143
Moses, 29, 31, 52
  and the oral Torah, 138
  five books of, 31, 32, 50, 51, 73,
    135, 165, 167
  foresaw time of restoration,
    13, 28, 163
  Torah given through, 72
  warns about false prophets,
    160
  wrote down the
    commandments, 136

N

Natural Law, 58, 59, 61, 63, 64,
  65
Nazarenes, 20
Nazis, 7
new creation, 69, 70, 71, 81, 82
new moon, 89, 97, 98, 102
New Testament, 14, 19, 24, 25,
  49, 50, 51, 52, 54, 75
  and the Torah, 47

O

oral Torah, 135, 136, 137, 138
  and believers, 144
  and Paul, 151
  and Yeshua, 142, 143
  hand washing, 139
  value of, 141, 142

P

Passover, 20, 24, 25, 82, 90, 91,
  92, 98, 99, 106, 109, 141
Paul, 22, 23, 145, 148
  and Gentile believers, 15, 18,
    86, 156
  and Peter, 10
  and Shavuot, 94
  and the Ephesians, 21
  and the Festivals, 97, 98
  and the Galatians, 153
  and the Passover, 91, 92
  and the Romans, 30
  and the Sabbath, 79, 84, 98
  and the Torah, 29, 31, 32, 33,
    40, 41, 49, 50, 52, 53, 54,
    59, 129, 147, 151
  and Timothy, 30
  imitating Yeshua, 155, 156
  in context, 157
  man of Torahlessness, 156
  martyred, 15
  ministry of, 14, 148
  the Pharisee, 150

writings of, 11, 12, 18, 19, 41,
    50, 128, 153, 167, 171
Pentecost. *See* Shavuot
Peter, 22, 73, 79, 94
  and Gentile believers, 10
  and Paul, 10
  martyred, 15
Pharisees, 11, 14, 42, 82, 84, 87,
    121, 140, 141, 143, 144
  and handwashing, 139
Protestant Reformation, 23, 24
purity laws, 127, 129

R

Rabbis
  Akiva, 17, 39, 40
  Hillel, 37, 38, 39, 45, 144
  Shammai, 37, 38, 39, 45, 144
Reformation, 22, 23, 24
repentance, 53, 76, 99, 123, 160
Replacement Theology, 18
Roman Empire, 16, 19
  Nero, 15
  Vespasian, 15
Rule of Law, 114, 118, 119, 120,
    121

S

Sabbath, 7, 8, 16, 64, 75, 78, 80,
    89, 90, 98, 106, 109, 118,
    125, 127, 131, 133, 154,
    166
  and Sunday, 6, 20, 24, 83
  a shadow, 78, 79
  day of peace, 79
  disciples observed, 85, 86, 147,
    153
  Gentiles observed, 86
  observance forbidden, 18, 20,
    24, 77
  observance of, 10, 18, 24, 79,
    81, 83, 145
  the seventh day, 6
  traditions, 78, 82, 109, 145

Yeshua's observance, 47, 48,
    78, 84, 87, 142
sacrifices, 76, 102, 123, 127,
    130, 133, 150
Scripture(s), 35, 49, 54, 152
  Canon of, 50
  interpretation of, 24, 51, 128
  is God-breathed, 31
  priority of, 8, 52
  the weight of, 138
second century, 17, 111, 135,
    136, 138
Second Jewish Revolt.
    See Jewish Wars
Shavuot, 90, 93, 98, 104, 110
sin, 44, 54, 67, 69, 72, 82, 87, 91,
    126, 131
  confession, atonement, 95
  definition of, 29, 30, 42, 121
Sinai, 32, 33, 34, 35, 45, 55, 57,
    58, 60, 61, 64, 65, 73, 93,
    94, 98, 107, 135, 136, 139
slavery, 35, 91, 125, 127, 130
Solomon, 113, 115, 118
Sukkot. *See* Festival of Booths

T

Talmud, 9, 32, 83, 136, 137, 138,
    140, 143, 165
tefillin, 106
telos. *See* goal
Teshuvah movement, 2
Torah
  a reflection of Messiah, 59, 61,
    68
  beauty of, 109, 151
  community, 172
  covenants of, 32, 33, 45, 52
  definition of, 135
  like a builder's cubit, 37, 38, 45
  like a ketubah, 34, 35
  made flesh, 44, 72, 142
  prophetic return to, 1, 13, 27,

163, 164
reading cycle, 48, 166
revelation of God, 8, 52, 57, 58,
61, 73
soul mirror, 67, 68, 73
summary of, 40, 41
written on our hearts, 33, 63,
69
Torah Club, 133, 157, 165
tzitzit, 105

U

United Nations, 2, 27
Unleavened Bread. *See* Passover

Y

Yad V'Shem, 6
Yeshua. *See also* oral Torah
and breaking the Sabbath, 82
and the oral Torah, 142
attitude toward Torah, 14, 31,
39, 40, 44, 115, 120
the Living Torah, 73, 146
the Torah made flesh, 44, 72,
142

ENDNOTES

CHAPTER 1

[1] Jerusalem University College

[2] Galatians 2:14

CHAPTER 2

[3] Romans 11:17

[4] Ephesians 2:12-13

[5] Ephesians 3:6

[6] O'Quinn, Chris "Fiscus Judaicus," *Bikurei Tzion*, #72, p. 28.

[7] b.*Berachot* 28b–29a.

[8] Pseudo-Ignatius, *Epistle to the Magnesians*

[9] Justin Martyr, *Dialogue with Trypho*, chapter 47.

[10] Tertullian, *Against Marcion*, 4.5.

[11] Eusebius, *Life of Constantine*, v. 3, c. 18-19.

[12] Chrysostom, John, *Against the Jews,* Homily 1.5.

[13] Weiner, Peter F., *Martin Luther, Hitler's Spiritual Ancestor,* Hutchinson & Co. Ltd., London: New York: Melbourne: Sydney. Online version at www.tentmaker.org/books/MartinLuther-HitlersSpiritualAncestor.html#jews

CHAPTER 3

[14] Romans 3:23

[15] 1 Corinthians 14:21

[16] John 10:34; 15:25

[17] For more information about the oral traditions, oral law and the *Talmud*, see Chapter 14.

[18] Ephesians 2:12

[19] Genesis 9

[20] Exodus 29:9

21 Numbers 25:11–13

22 Exodus 24:7

23 Exodus 24:7

24 Encyclopedia Judaica, "Covenant," Vol. 5.

25 For example, *Exodus Rabbah* 46:1.

CHAPTER 4

26 b.*Shabbat* 31a.

27 Lachs, Samuel Tobias, *A Rabbinic Commentary on the New Testament*, Ktav Publishing House, Inc. (1987), p. 281.

28 Mark 12:30–31

29 1 John 3:4

30 *Avodah Zarah* 8b. Edersheim, *Jesus the Messiah* (1993), p. 858.

31 m.*Makkot* 1:10.

32 Deuteronomy 17:6

33 Cohen, Abraham, *Everyman's Talmud*, Schocken Books (1975), p. 307.

34 O.T. Apocrypha of Daniel 14. The Book of Susanna.

CHAPTER 5

35 m.*Megillah* 4.2.

36 In modern practice, the reader called to read from the prophets is actually an eighth reader of Torah in that he reads the last few verses of the Torah (*maftir*) before beginning to read from the prophets. In the days of the Apostles, the seventh reader probably filled this role.

37 John 5:39

38 Matthew 4:4

39 Matthew 27:46

40 Luke 24:44–45

41 Acts 25:8, 28:17

42 Hebrews 4:15

43 Moseley, Dr. Ron, *Yeshua: A Guide to the Real Jesus and the Original Church*, Messianic Jewish Publishers (1996), p. 39.

44 Isaiah 42:1–4, 21, cf. Matthew 12:18–21

45 Acts 7:38

46 Hebrews 10:7

47 2 Corinthians 3:12–18

48 2 Timothy 3:16–17

49 Luke 24:44

50 Galatians 3:15–17

51 Deuteronomy 13

52 For example, Ezekiel 14:6; 18:30

53 For example, Isaiah 2:3; Jeremiah 31:33–34

54 For example, Proverbs 28:4, 9; 29:18

55 For example, Psalm 119

56 Matthew 4:17

57 For example, Matthew 5:17; Mark 7:9

58 For example, Matthew 5; 12:5; 22:32

59 Matthew 5:17–19

60 Revelations 12:17, 14:12

61 Deuteronomy 13

62 2 Timothy 3:16

CHAPTER 6

63 Exodus 20:2

64 For example, *The Abolition of Man; Mere Christianity.*

65 Tim Hegg, author of *The Letter Writer* and FFOZ theological editorial chairman, in personal communication pointed out another, more probable reading of Romans 2 which suggests that the Gentiles with the Torah written on their hearts of which Paul is speaking are actually believers, not heathens, for this is the promise of the new covenant in Jeremiah 31. "I will put My law within them and on their heart I will write it." (Jeremiah 31:33) Nevertheless, the conventional reading of Romans 2 understands the passage to speak of Natural Law, a concept that is supported by other passages.

66 Ezekiel 36:27–28

67 Galatians 5:22–23

CHAPTER 7

68 Berkowitz, *Torah Rediscovered*, First Fruits of Zion (1996), p. 85.

69 Matthew 7:24–27

70 Clement of Alexandria, *Strom*, 1.29.182.

CHAPTER 8

71 Matthew 5:17–20; John 14:15–21

72 Acts 21:20

73 Leviticus 17, Deuteronomy 12

74 70 and 135 CE respectively.

75 Colossians 2:16–17

76 Colossians 2:16–17

77 For example, b.*Sanhedrin* 97a.

78 Deuteronomy 5:15

[79] For full discussions of the Talmudic parallels to Jesus' Sabbath arguments, see FFOZ's *Torah Club Volume Four*.

[80] Revelation 1:10

[81] Luke 4:16

[82] Leviticus 23:3

[83] Luke 15:1

[84] John 5:17

[85] Matthew 24:20

[86] Exodus 20:8–10; Isaiah 56:3–6; 66:23

[87] Acts 15:21

Chapter 9

[88] Leviticus 23:10–11

[89] *Menachot* 10:3. See *Mishnah, Menachot* 10 for detailed information on the omer ritual.

[90] B.*Shabbat* 88b; e.g., *Shemot Rabbah* 5:9. Weissman, Moshe, *The Midrash Says, Shemos*, Bnai Yaakov Publications (1995), p. 182, *citing Midrash Chazit*. To study the matter thoroughly, read FFOZ's *The Mystery of the Gospel*.

[91] Acts 20:16

[92] Leviticus 23:42–43

[93] Micah 4:4; Zechariah 3:10

[94] Isaiah 4:5–6

Chapter 10

[95] See the laws of Leviticus 15 and 18.

[96] Leviticus 15:5-14, 31

[97] Romans 6:3–5

[98] Matthew 9:20; Mark 6:56

[99] Deuteronomy 6:9

[100] Deuteronomy 6:8

[101] For further study, you may want to consider FFOZ's *Holy Cow!*, and *Torah* Club *Volumes One, Four and Five*.

[102] Encyclopedia Judaica, "Purity Laws," Vol. 14, p. 1409.

[103] Genesis 8:15–9:13

[104] Deuteronomy 6:4-9

[105] Marcion's Heresy, see chapter 1.

Chapter 11

[106] *Exodus Rabbah* 6:1.

107 Can we really draw a correlation between the words of Yeshua and a third-century *midrash*? It is a common error of critical scholarship to assume that the body of *Midrash* (written between the second and the fifth centuries) is younger than the Gospels. The strength of the oral tradition is well attested within the early centuries of Rabbinic Judaism and a couple of centuries is a short span for oral transmission. That many later recorded *midrashim* are concurrent and even predate the Gospels is evident from the Apostolic Scriptures' and early *Targums'* frequent uses of and allusions to various *midrashic* traditions.

108 Bonhoeffer, Deitrich, *The Cost of Discipleship*, Collier Books, MacMillan Publishing (1959).

CHAPTER 12

109 Although the author of the letter cites Leviticus 10:10 as his proof text, the text he had in mind was probably Deuteronomy 14:3. Subsequent versions of the letter have been corrected.

110 Idolatry: Deuteronomy 7:25; 13:14; 17:1-4; 20:18. Child sacrifice: 12:31. Divination, sorcery, witchcraft, spell casting, channeling spirits and consulting the dead: 18:10–12. Prostitution in worship: 23:18. Cross-dressing: 22:5. Re-remarriage: 24:4. False weights and measures: 25:15-16.

111 Romans 1:26–27 springs to mind.

112 Deuteronomy 12:13–14

113 Acts 2:46; 3:1; 5:42; 21:26; 25:8

114 See Hope Egan's *Holy Cow!*, FFOZ (2005) for more on the dietary laws and a discussion of the relevant passages from the Apostolic Scriptures.

115 Deuteronomy 12:13–14. Beyond any doubt, the death of the Messiah is foreshadowed in the sacrifices, and He is our atoning sacrifice in the eternal Temple which is above. Yet the early believers continued in the Temple rites until its destruction.

CHAPTER 13

116 The Mark 7 passage is more extensively explored in First Fruits of Zion's *Holy Cow!* This exegesis is borrowed, in part, from that work and *Torah Club Volume Four* on Mark 7.

117 Numbers 19

118 m.*Yadayim* 2:4.

119 Rabbi Abbahu's opinion in *Sotah* 5a citing Ezekiel 4:13.

120 Deuteronomy 8:10

121 m.*Avot* 3:5; b.*Berachot* 12b; b.*Yoma* 85b; b.*Yevamoth* 47b; b.*Sanhedrin* 94b and others.

122 This is the yoke Peter refers to in Acts 15.

123   The Shem Tov reading on Matthew 23:2–3 popularized in Nehemia Gordon's *The Hebrew Yeshua vs. the Greek Jesus - New light on the seat of Moses from Shem-Tov's Hebrew Matthew* is not a reliable reading of that text. Aside from the fact that it comes from a spurious, medieval manuscript that contradicts far more ancient readings of the verse, the purported wording appears only in a minority of extant of Shem Tov manuscripts, suggesting a scribal error, not a valid textual variant.

124   Exodus 35:3

CHAPTER 14

125   Acts 15:19–20; 21:25

126   Acts 18:18

127   The Greek word *telos* is better translated as "goal" than "end."

128   In Jewish literature, the term "good work" or "good deed" is synonymous with the term "commandment" (*mitzvah*).

129   In Torah and later Jewish literature, the term "the commandment" is a synonym for Torah.

130   In Jewish literature, the term "good work" or "good deed" is synonymous with the term "commandment" (*mitzvah*).

131   1 Corinthians 7:18

132   Galatians 2:3

133   See Acts 15, Romans 14, Colossians 2 and Galatians 2–4.

134   Matthew 5:17-20

CHAPTER 15

135   Deuteronomy 18:20–22

136   b.*Sanhedrin* 43a.

137   This story is told in *Oznayim LaTorah* and cited in Weissman's *The Midrash Says, Devarim*, Benei Yaakov Publications (1985), p. 172.

APPENDIX

138   m.*Peah* 1:1.

139   There is every indication that Israeli Jewry read the Torah on a triennial cycle in the days of the Master, but for the past 1,600 years or so, the annual cycle has been favored.

ADDITIONAL RESOURCES

Did *Restoration* leave you with more questions than answers? Don't despair! First Fruits of Zion publishes many resources that will help you learn even more about God's Word.

FIRST FRUITS OF ZION

BIBLE STUDY PROGRAMS, BOOKS AND TEACHINGS MATERIAL

Do you want to understand God's Word in its historical, cultural and linguistic context? First Fruits of Zion resources will help you better understand the Bible.

◊ **Restoration Workbook and 6 CD Audio Book**

Host a *Restoration* Bible study in your home or fellowship. By using this helpful companion workbook and Audio CDs, you can help share the beauty of Torah life with your family friends. Contains flexible chapter/sections idea for scheduling a four, eight or sixteen-week study.

◊ **Messiah magazine**

Published five times a year, each full-color issue provides fresh articles and perspectives about our Torah-observant Messiah, the grace we have in Him, and the truth He taught. For more information or to subscribe, visit *www.messiahmagazine.org*.

◊ King of the Jews
Resurrecting the Jewish Jesus

Bible critics and scholars are talking about the difference between the Jesus Christ of Christianity and the historical Jesus. But who is the historical Jesus? He is not a one-size-fits-all mystic. He wasn't a Christian either. Jesus was a Jew. *King of the Jews* digs into the history and literature of early Judaism to demonstrate the authenticity of the Gospels and to dispel today's errant re-interpretations of Jesus.

◊ The Letter Writer
Paul's Background and Torah Perspective

This book by Tim Hegg challenges traditional Christian viewpoints of Paul, his message, and the foundation of his theological approach. Through this book, Hegg re-establishes a biblical, historical and cultural understanding of Paul—the Torah observant Apostle.

◊ Fellowheirs
Jews & Gentiles Together in the Family of God.

A masterful piece of scholarship! This book seeks the biblical perspective on identity within the family of God. Is the Torah for all of God's children, or is it only for Jews? The powerful results of Tim Hegg's research demonstrate from the biblical text that Jews and Gentiles are both beholden to the same covenant norms and responsibilities.

◊ The Mystery of the Gospel
Jew and Gentile and the Eternal Purpose of God

Addressing the question of Jewish/Gentile relationships within the body of Messiah, D. Thomas Lancaster works through the Apostle Paul's rabbinic scholarship to piece together the deep mystery of the Messiah, about the identity of Gentile believers and their relationship to Israel through the Messiah.

◊ **Holy Cow!**

Does God Care About what We Eat?

Join best-selling author Hope Egan on her personal journey through what the Bible says about eating meat. See how science and Scripture brilliantly intertwine. Promoting neither legalism nor vegetarianism, Holy Cow! gently challenges you to take a fresh look at how you live out your faith!

◊ **HaYesod**

This 14-week video Bible study delves into the Hebraic roots of Christianity and is ideal for group teaching or personal study. For more information visit *www.hayesod.org* or call 800-775-4807 and request a HaYesod info pack.

◊ **Torah Club**

Study the Torah, the Gospels and Acts passage-by-passage from within the context of Torah and classical Judaism. It is FFOZ's most comprehensive resource for providing biblical context. Visit *www.torahclub.org* or call toll free 800-775-4807 to request a brochure.

WWW.FFOZ.ORG   WWW.MYFFOZ.ORG

For more information about these and other FFOZ books, magazines and multi-media products, or to download free samples, please visit *www.ffoz.org* or call toll free 800-775-4807.

◊ **Premium Online Content—FREE**

FFOZ provides additional online content and services to Myffoz members. Anyone who joins will receive access to premium online content, including the Weekly eDrash, the Monthly eRosh, and Magazine articles. To join, go to *www.myffoz.org.*

Visit the FFOZ's online webstore to securely purchase any of these and other resources. Go to *www.ffoz.org/store.*